Abraham and David

Places They Knew

by

F. F. Bruce

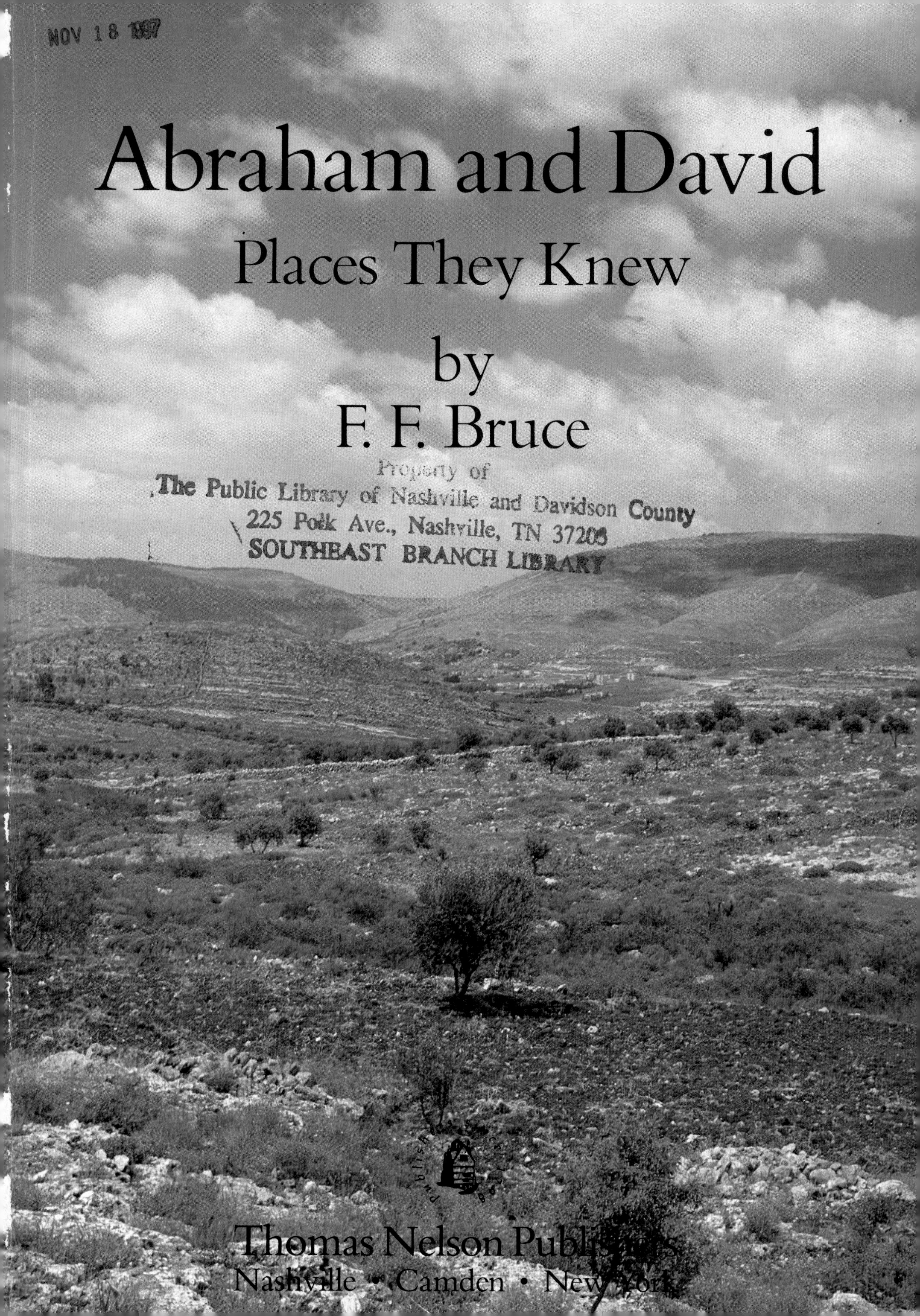

Thomas Nelson Publishers
Nashville • Camden • New York

The Ancient Near East

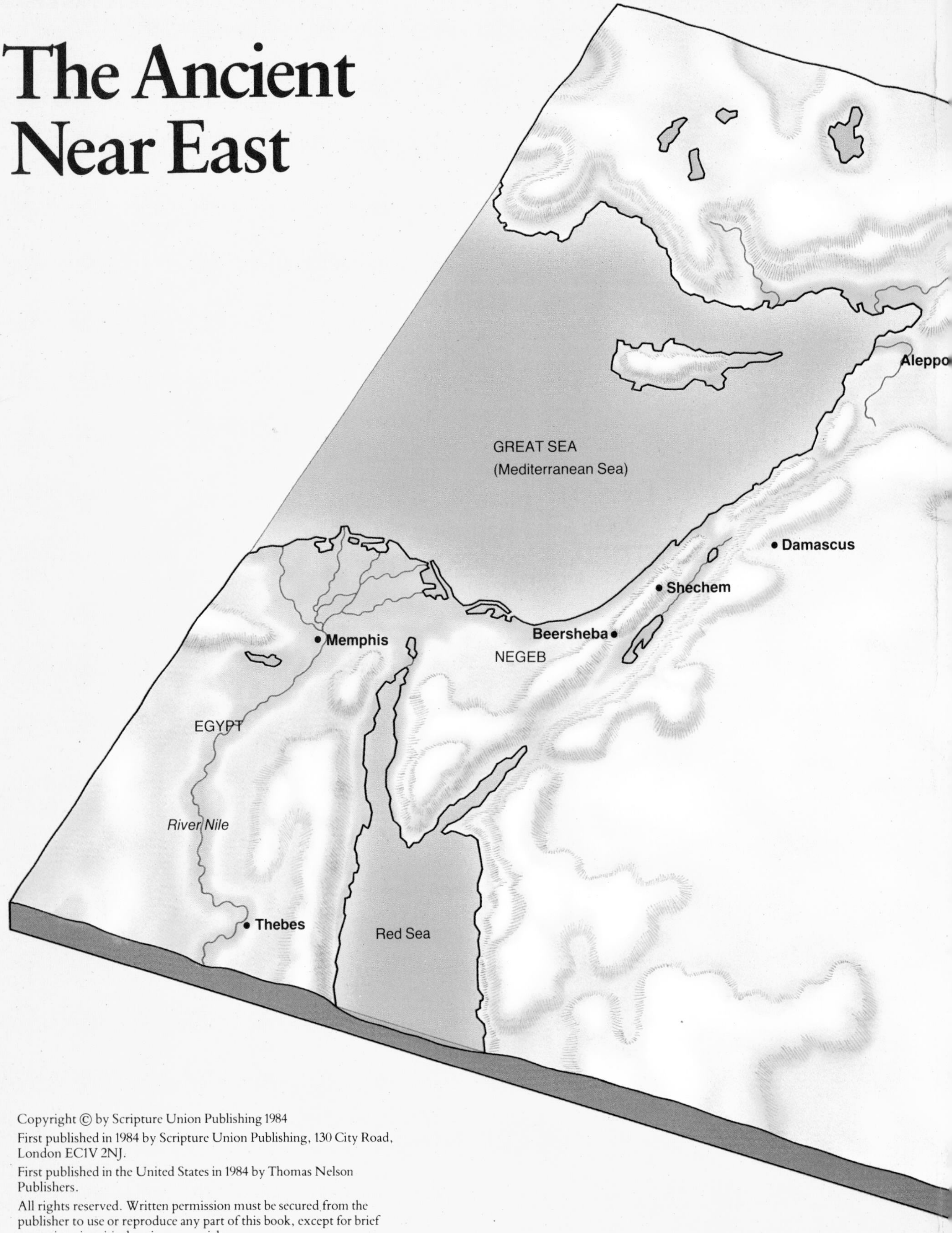

First published in 1984 by Scripture Union Publishing, 130 City Road, London EC1V 2NJ.

First published in the United States in 1984 by Thomas Nelson Publishers.

Published in Nashville, Tennessee, by Thomas Nelson, Inc. and distributed in Canada by Lawson Falle, Ltd., Cambridge, Ontario.

ISBN 0-8407-5402-7

Printed in Italy

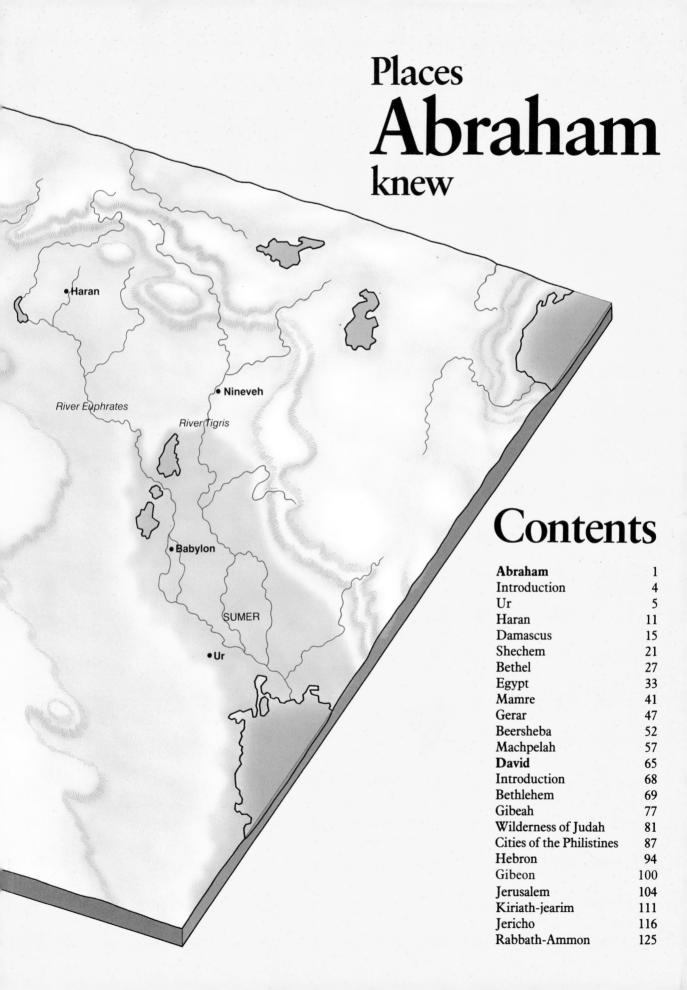

Places Abraham knew

Contents

Introduction

This is a companion volume to *Places They Knew: Jesus and Paul*. There is nothing strange about linking Abraham and David together in one volume: they are linked together in the first verse of the New Testament, where Jesus Christ is called 'the son of David, the son of Abraham'.

The people and events described in the Bible were very much down-to-earth; they did not belong to some never-never land beyond the clouds. Some of the men and women whom we meet in the Bible lived all their lives in the same place; many others travelled widely. It is remarkable how many of the outstanding figures of the Bible story were travellers, constantly on the move. If we can envisage them in their various geographical settings, it helps us to understand many of the things that are recorded about them.

Many features of the Bible lands have changed between those earlier days and our own, but not all. The Bedouin tents may still look much as they did in Abraham's time, but the people who live in them today keep in touch with domestic and international news with the aid of transistor radios; this gives them a different outlook on the world. However, we can still appreciate the difference between the wilderness where they live and the cultivated land which adjoins it, or the difference between country life and city life. Egypt's fertility still depends on the Nile, even if the flow is now regulated by the high dam above Aswan. Syria and the Holy Land still depend on seasonal rainfall for their harvests. The donkey and the camel are still used by some people for getting around, even if they have been supplemented by more rapid means of modern transport.

Human life was controlled by natural conditions in Bible days, and to a large extent it still is. To learn something, therefore, of the places which the Bible characters knew is a great help to seeing their lives and actions in a proper context. The best way to learn, no doubt, is to visit the places ourselves and picture the persons and events associated with them. But if that cannot be done, then photographs and verbal descriptions will do something to fill the gap. Some of the places are still busy centres of human activity; others have been excavated after being covered over for centuries, and stand as relics of what once was. Either way, they can teach us something about the Bible story. It is to provide this kind of commentary on the Bible story that these volumes are issued.

February 1984

F. F. BRUCE

Ur

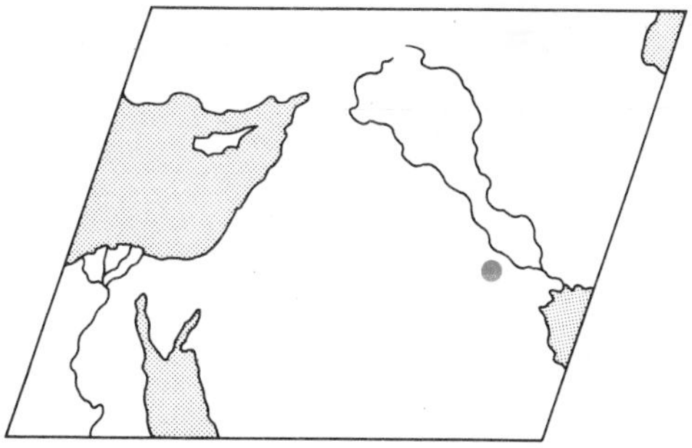

Ur of the Chaldees was the place from which Abraham and his family set out on the journey which brought them ultimately to Canaan. The Chaldees were originally a nomadic group in the desert between North Arabia and the Persian Gulf, which migrated to Southern Babylonia and settled there.

If Abraham's Ur is rightly identified with the ancient city of that name in Southern Babylonia, marked today by the mound of Tell Muqayyar (and no other identification is so probable), then the culture which Abraham gave up for the nomadic way of life which he was thenceforth to pursue was a highly sophisticated urban civilization.

Ur was a religious centre, dedicated to the worship of the moon-god, who was called Sin in Akkadian (the Semitic language of Babylonia) and Nanna or Nannar in the ancient Sumerian language. To the moon-god was consecrated an extensive

Archaeological excavations in North Syria, near the River Euphrates. This Sumerian site dates from the 2nd and 3rd millennia BC.

This skeleton excavated in Babylonia, Iraq dates from the Sumerian period. The remains of a shell belt can be seen in addition to the human bones.

temple area in the city centre, called Ekishnugal; within this area stood the ziggurat or terrace-tower Etemeniguru, built by Ur-nammu, founder of the third dynasty of Ur, about 2100 B.C. The ziggurat stood on a base of 200 by 150 feet; it was reconstructed by Nabonidus, the last king of Babylon, about 550 B.C. The daughter of Nabonidus served as priestess of the moon-god in Ur. We do not know if Abraham in his early days was a worshipper of the moon-god; what we do know is that he had a revelation from the living and true God which taught him to dismiss all thought of the many gods of his native culture. 'The God of glory', said Stephen, 'appeared to our father Abraham.' What form this revelation took, apart from the command to leave his home for a destination unknown, we are not told, but it was sufficient to give a new course to the rest of Abraham's life.

A shepherd with his flock on the banks of the River Euphrates north of Al Thaura, North Syria.

The site of ancient Ur was explored by J. E. Taylor in 1854 and by R. C. Thompson and H. R. Hall in 1918 and the following years. Then, between 1922 and 1934, it was thoroughly excavated by a joint expedition from the British Museum and the Museum of the University of Pennsylvania, directed by Sir Leonard Woolley. From their explorations the following outline of the history of the city emerges.

Like other parts of Southern Babylonia, Ur received its first human settlement about 4300 B.C. In the history of culture this is known as the Al-'Ubaid period, after the name of a place about four miles north of Ur, where the first remains of this culture were discovered. The Al-'Ubaid period lasted for nearly a thousand years. Towards the end of this period Ur suffered from a great inundation, evidence of which was preserved in a bed of water-laid clay. The eight- to eleven feet of sediment, said Sir Leonard Woolley when the discovery was made, 'imply a very great depth of water, and the flood which deposited it must have been of a magnitude unparalleled in local

A wooden-wheeled wagon pulled by asses, from the famous Standard of Ur.

history'. He believed, indeed, that this must have been the flood described in the Genesis story of Noah; this, however, is far from certain.

In any case, the great flood of Ur marked a definite break in the continuity of the local culture. The painted pottery, for example, characteristic of the Al-'Ubaid period, suddenly and completely disappears: 'the people who made it', according to Woolley, 'were wiped out by the Flood'.

Ur was resettled after the flood by Sumerians, under whom it attained a high level of material and intellectual culture. Its political significance begins about 2500 B.C. To this period belongs what is commonly called the royal cemetery of Ur, in which an amazing wealth of equipment and adornment of gold, silver and precious stones was found buried with the dead. Although the dead cannot be certainly identified with royalty, it is difficult to suppose that such wealth belonged to people of less than royal status. For all the high level of civilization to which the burials bear witness, the bodies of human victims, sacrificed to wait on their masters and mistresses in the after-life, indicate that the civilization had some way to go in the matter of human rights. One man, whose name is unknown, was buried with sixty-three helmeted soldiers, grooms and gold-garlanded girls, not to mention two chariots and six bullocks. One of the most exquisite masterpieces was a richly ornamented harp from the tomb of a lady called Shubad. Most fascinating of all the finds, in the eyes of many, was the 'standard of Ur' – a pictorial mosaic 1 foot 7 inches long by 8½ inches high, with three registers running the whole length on both sides, depicting scenes of war and peace, 'a masterpiece of early Sumerian art', as D. J. Wiseman justly calls it. The public impact of the discovery of these tombs and their contents was not unlike the impact made by the discovery of Tutankhamun's tomb in Egypt, four years earlier, in 1922.

Three royal dynasties of Ur are mentioned in the ancient king-lists, beginning about 2375 B.C. It was under the third of these (2047-1939 B.C.) that Ur became the leading city in Southern Mesopotamia. At this time it covered a roughly oval area about five furlongs in length and three in breadth. It was surrounded by a wall and, on three of its sides, by water also – by an arm of the Euphrates and a canal. It had two harbours, for the Euphrates was navigable to seaborne vessels and Ur traded, through the Persian Gulf, with foreign lands and thus grew very rich.

Ur-nammu, first king of the third dynasty, was the author of a law-code which, when it was discovered in 1952, was the oldest law-code known up to that time. Ur, at this date, was the greatest commercial capital that the world had yet seen; the thousands of business documents from this period, says W. F. Albright, 'include an elaborate system of double-entry book-keeping'.

Shrines to various deities were set up at the intersections of the narrow streets. From those streets one passed into private houses which were exceptionally well appointed. In conformity with a pattern common in the Near East throughout biblical times, the entrance from the street led into a paved court surrounded on three sides by rooms. There were cooking, washing and toilet facilities, with a private chapel and storage space. An upper floor was supported on arches. If Abraham lived in such a house, his subsequent life as a tent-dweller must have called for considerable adjustment.

The third dynasty of Ur came to an end under attacks from Elam on the east and incursions by Amorites from the west. We have no incontrovertible evidence for the date of Abraham, but his departure from Ur could have taken place in the troubled period following the end of the third dynasty.

After this date Ur never regained its political power, although after its rebuilding it continued to be an important centre. It retained its religious significance for many centuries. But in the Bible its significance lies in the fact that it was the city which Abraham forsook because, as we are

Sumerian jewellery from Ur. The jewellery has been arranged as it was discovered in a tomb dating from about 2500 BC.

Cutaway reconstruction of a two-storey house at Ur.

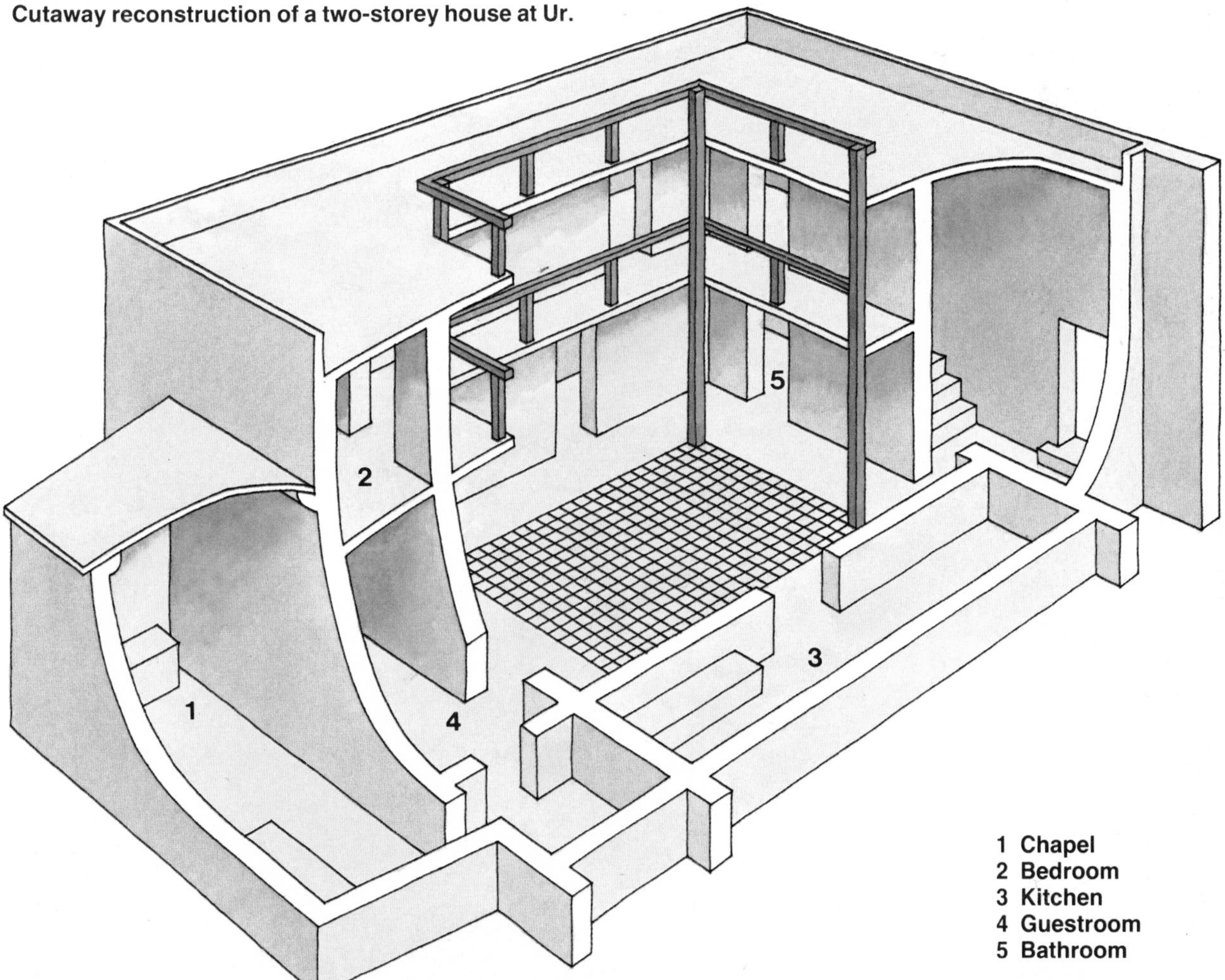

1 Chapel
2 Bedroom
3 Kitchen
4 Guestroom
5 Bathroom

These Sumerian necklaces from around 2500 BC are made of gold, lapis lazuli and carnelian.

assured in the New Testament, 'he looked forward to the city which has foundations, whose builder and maker is God' (Heb. 11.10).

Biblical references Genesis 11.27-30 – Abraham's family in Ur.
Genesis 11.31 – Abraham's family leaves Ur; no reason stated.
Genesis 15.7 – Abraham is reminded in a vision that it was the Lord who brought him from Ur to the promised land.
Nehemiah 9.7 – Fifteen centuries later the descendants of Abraham remember that it was God who chose Abraham and brought him out of Ur, and that he has remained faithful throughout to the promises he made to Abraham and his posterity.
Acts 7.2, 3 – Stephen declares that the God of glory appeared to Abraham when he lived in the land of the Chaldaeans and gave him his marching orders. Such a revelation explains much that was otherwise inexplicable in Abraham's conduct.
Hebrews 11.8, 10 – The revelation that Abraham received included the vision of the city of God. For the sake of that well-founded and eternal city one might well abandon any earthly city.

Artist's reconstruction of the ziggurat at Ur

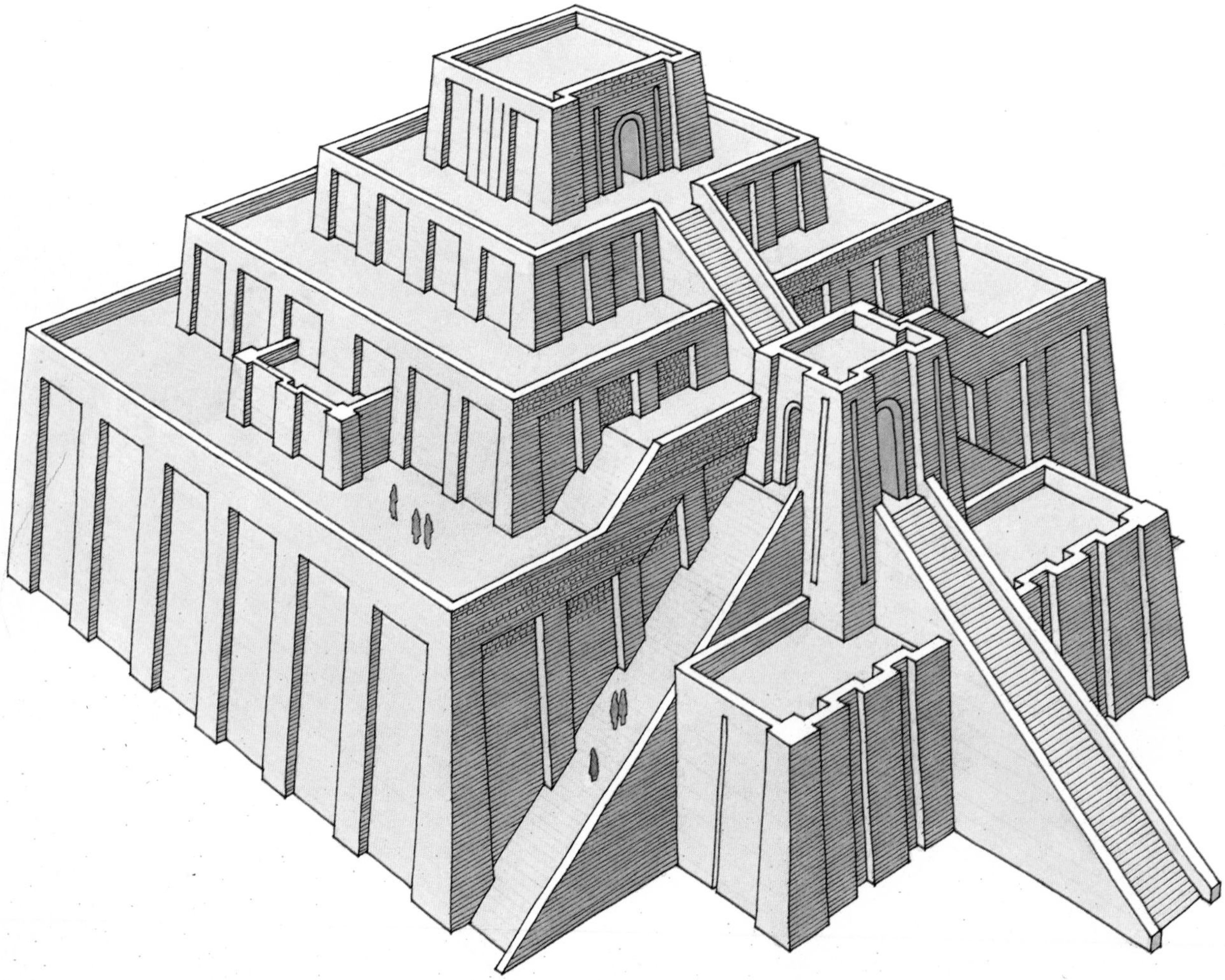

Haran

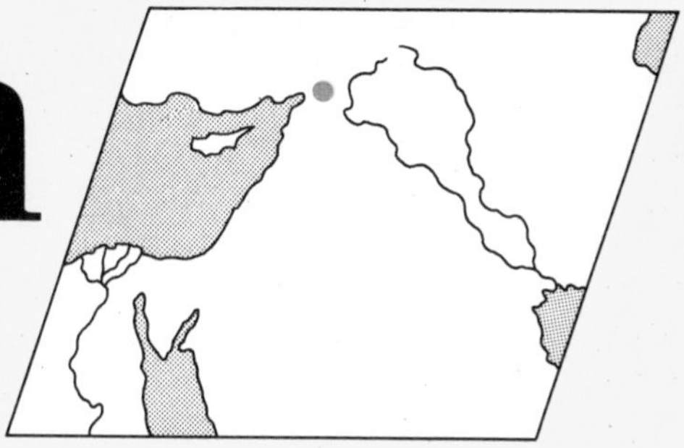

Haran (better spelt Harran) was the place at which Abraham and his family halted for some time on their journey from Ur of the Chaldees. Here Terah, Abraham's father, died and after his death Abraham, with his wife Sarah and his nephew Lot, 'and the persons that they had gotten in Haran', set out to continue their journey to Canaan. If we had only Gen. 11.31 to guide us, we might conclude that it was Terah who took the initiative in the family's departure from Ur, but this may simply indicate that he receives the honour due to him as head of the family. We are left in no doubt that it was Abraham who took the initiative in the departure from Haran, in response to a divine command and promise. Some members of the family stayed on in Haran or its vicinity. It was to the neighbouring city of Nahor that Abraham's servant went to find a wife for Isaac among his kinsfolk (Gen. 24.10), and it was to Haran that

The modern village of Haran in south-east Turkey stands within the area occupied by the ancient city which Abraham knew.

Jacob, in the next generation, went to escape the vengeance of Esau and served for twenty years with Laban, his mother's brother (Gen. 27.43; 28.10; 29.4).

Haran lies on the river Balikh, which flows into the upper Euphrates from the east. It thus belongs to Mesopotamia in the strict sense of that term, 'between the rivers' (Euphrates and Tigris). The site now lies in Turkey, about twelve miles north of the border with Syria. Nearby is the town still called Haran (about twenty miles south-east of Urfa, the ancient Edessa); the site of Old Testament Haran is marked by the ruins of Eski-haran ('Old Haran'), a little way north-west of the modern town.

The name of the city is Akkadian in origin: *harranu* means 'main road' or 'cross-roads'. It was so called because it lay on an important intersection on the caravan routes which ran north from southern

The citadel of Aleppo, North Syria, where Abraham is said to have camped during his journey from Ur to Haran.

A desert scene near Palmyra (Tadmor) in Syria. The ridges are in the heart of the great Syrian desert.

Babylonia and then west into Asia Minor or south-west into Syria and so on to Egypt. Despite the resemblance in English, the name of the city is not identical with that of Abraham's brother Haran (Lot's father). Abraham's brother Haran died before the family left Ur (Gen. 11.28) and had nothing to do with the city of Haran.

Haran, like Ur, was a centre of the cult of the moon-god. Perhaps his temple at Haran, Ehulhul, was founded by kings of the third dynasty of Ur; but there is no reason to think that it was this religious association between Ur and Haran that made Haran a natural halting-place for Abraham and his family on their way from Ur. Under the third dynasty of Ur that city engaged actively in regular trade with Haran, and through Haran with more distant places. The trade which the Old Assyrian kingdom carried on with Cappadocia, as far back as about 1950 B.C., would also have passed through Haran, as well as Assyrian and Iranian trade with Syria and Egypt.

Haran is first mentioned in cuneiform records of Cappadocia in the nineteenth century B.C. A little later it appears in texts from Mari (on the Middle Euphrates), which also mention the city of Nahor. Its destruction by the Assyrians in 763 B.C. is mentioned in 2 Kings 19.12 (paralleled in Isa. 37.12). It was rebuilt by Sargon II (721-

In biblical times, the camel was not merely a vital means of transport but also a symbol of a man's wealth.

Haran 705 B.C.), and when Nineveh fell in 612 B.C., Haran became, for the next two years, the last capital of the Assyrian Empire. It then became a Babylonian city: King Nabonidus (556-539 B.C.) patronized the temple of the moon-god at Haran as well as his temple at Ur. As his daughter was high-priestess of the moon-god at Ur, so his mother was high-priestess at Haran, until her death at the age of 104. In Greek and Roman times the place was known as Carrhae: here the Parthians, who ruled the territory east of the Euphrates, inflicted a disastrous defeat on an invading Roman army under Crassus in 53 B.C.

In 1951 an Anglo-Turkish expedition began an archaeological exploration of the site, and uncovered an important library of cuneiform texts from the late Assyrian period. In 1956 a later expedition found some inscribed stelae from the late Babylonian period, including two of Nabonidus and one of his mother.

Biblical references Genesis 11.32 – 'Terah died in Haran'. It is implied here, and stated in Acts 7.4, that Abraham did not continue his journey from Haran to the promised land until his father had died.

Can any reason be suggested for his doing so?

Genesis 12.5 – Abraham and his companions are said to have taken with them on their journey 'the persons that they had gotten in Haran'. Consider the suggestion that these 'persons' ('souls' in AV) were not simply members of their family or household servants, but men and women whom they had won over to faith in the God of Abraham, and who said, 'Let us go with you, for we have heard that God is with you' (compare Zechariah 8.23).

All dates are BC, and approximate.

2225
Terah born

2166
Abram (Abraham) born

2116
Abram migrates to Haran

2091
Abram enters Canaan

2066
Isaac born

Biblical events

Contemporary events

Gutian rule in Babylonia (2250-2120)
Third Dynasty of Ur arises to power in Abraham's birthplace (2113-2006)

First Intermediate Period (Dark Ages) in Egypt (2181-2040)

Ur-Nammu, Dungi, Bur-Sin, Gimil-Sin and Ibi-Sin rule at Ur. Trade between Ur, Haran, Damascus and Egypt

2080 Invasion of Transjordan by coalition of Mesopotamian kings (Genesis 14)

2056 Sodom and Gomorrah destroyed

Abraham's age

Damascus

Did Abraham know Damascus?
He could not have avoided knowing it: the main caravan road from Haran to Canaan passed through Damascus. Reference is made in Gen. 15.2 to 'Eliezer of Damascus' as heir to Abraham's house. He is probably the person described by Abraham in the next verse as 'a slave born in my house', who would be his heir in default of any children. The word 'slave' here translates an unusual Hebrew phrase, *ben mesheq*. Of

The Golan Heights, on the east shore of the Sea of Galilee, north-east Israel.

The Assyrians named the area in which Damascus stands 'the land of asses'.

the two components of this phrase *ben* is the common word for 'son' but we cannot be sure of the meaning of *mesheq*. It may, however, be identical with the second part of the place-name *dammesheq*, 'Damascus', occurring in verse 2. Some scholars have conjectured that Mesheq was an older form of Damascus, and that the expression in Gen. 15.3 should be rendered not 'a slave born in my house' but 'my Damascene heir'.

It was evidently customary for a childless man to adopt one of his household slaves, who would look after him in his old age and ultimately inherit his property. (This custom is attested for a later phase of the patriarchal period in a place called Nuzu, east of the Tigris, near the modern Kirkuk.) Provision might be made, however, for a child born subsequently to this deed of adoption to become the heir. Thus, when God said to Abraham, 'This man shall

The souk (market) in modern Damascus

The modern city of Damascus, Syria.

not be your heir; your own son shall be your heir' (Gen. 15.4), it was not implied that Abraham would be breaking law or convention by transferring the inheritance from Eliezer to the son that was yet to be born to himself.

There is another, quite incidental, reference to Damascus in the story of Abraham, in the record of his defeat of the four invading kings from the east, when he 'pursued them to Hobah, north of Damascus' (Gen. 14.15).

A closer association of Abraham with Damascus is attested by a citizen of that place in later days – Nicolas of Damascus, the friend and biographer of King Herod. He states in the fourth book of his *Universal History* that Abraham (whom he called Abrames) 'became king in Damascus' and describes him as 'an immigrant, who arrived with an army from the land above Babylon called the land of the Chaldeans. But after a short time he left this country also with his people and took up residence in the land which was then called Canaan and is now Judaea.' He adds that 'the name of Abrames is still held in honour in the district of Damascus, and a village is pointed out which is called after him: "Abrames' Dwelling".' For these statements by Nicolas of Damascus we are indebted to the Jewish historian Josephus, who quotes them. Nicolas probably reproduces a tradition current in his native city. A somewhat

The Suleiman Mosque in modern Damascus.

older contemporary of his, the Roman historian Pompeius Trogus, includes Abraham in a list of early kings of Damascus. We need not take the tradition of Abraham's kingship too seriously, but the persistence of the tradition does suggest that Abraham had some association with Damascus, and was remembered there centuries later.

Damascus lies in a well-watered and fruitful plain. It occupied a strategic position on the great highways of the region. People travelling south from Haran to Damascus might take one of three roads from there to the south or west: into Transjordan and south to Arabia, or west of the Lake of Galilee into Canaan, or on farther west to Acco and then down the Mediterranean seaboard towards Egypt. It was the road into Canaan that Abraham followed.

The district in which Damascus stands is known by the name of Apum in Egyptian texts of the nineteenth century B.C., and in tablets from Mari on the Middle Euphrates about a century later. The district was for long famous for the donkeys which were bred there: the Assyrians called it 'the land of asses'. The city itself stands on the Nahr Barada which flows from the Antilebanon range, while another stream, the Nahr el-A'waj, flows some way to the south. These two streams are generally identified with 'Abana and Pharpar, the rivers of Damascus', of which Naaman spoke so proudly (2 Kings 5.12); but both of them disappear in the semi-arid steppe to the east.

Damascus is commonly held to be the oldest continuously inhabited city in the world. The circumstances of its first occupation are unknown and the etymology of its name uncertain. In the earliest period in which we know of it it was, like most of its neighbours, an Amorite city. The third dynasty of Ur, which pushed its imperial rule up the Euphrates in the generations immediately preceding Abraham's time, did not extend its political sovereignty as far west as Damascus; but its commercial power may well have reached there, so that even in Damascus Abraham had not entirely escaped from the cultural influence of his native city. The cultural influence of Ur was waning, however, by the time Abraham passed that way.

About the time that the third dynasty of Ur fell, the kings of the twelfth dynasty of Egypt began their imperial advance into Palestine and Syria, especially Sesostris III (1878-1843 B.C.). Their power was felt along the Mediterranean coast of Syria through Byblus (modern Jebeil) as far as Ugarit (modern Ras Shamra), and it must certainly have extended along the great north road to Damascus. Then, when Egyptian power receded after the end of the twelfth dynasty (1786 B.C.), the power of the Hittite Empire in Asia Minor began to extend southward, ultimately reaching the river Orontes. Damascus was never subject to Hittite rule, but was exposed to Hittite influence.

An elderly religious man makes his way through the narrow streets of the old quarter of Damascus.

1 Sounding
2 Stepped trench
3 Stratified excavation

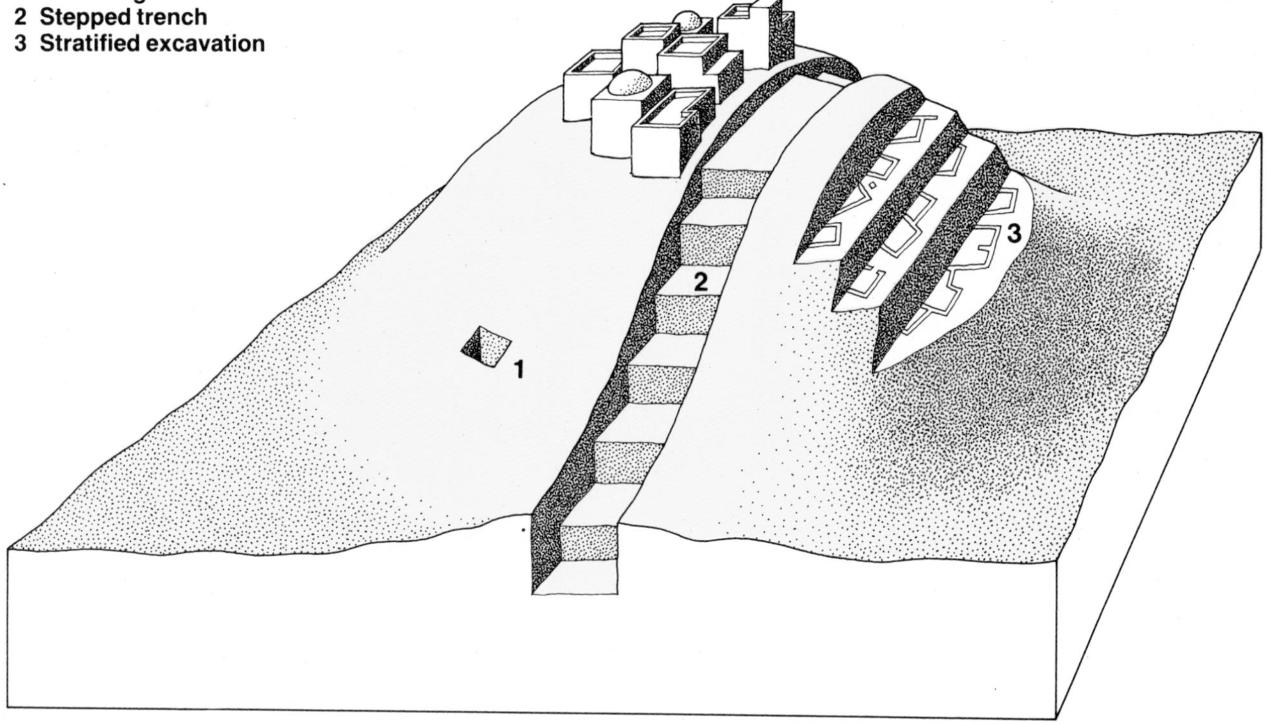

Diagram showing typical layers of successive occupation found during the archaeological excavation of a Tell.

A panel from the Black Obelisk showing subjects bringing tribute to Shalmaneser III of Assyria.

Egyptian military might was reasserted in that area by Thothmes III (1490-1436 B.C.), who conducted seventeen campaigns in Syria, reaching as far as the Euphrates. Indeed, the earliest known occurrence of the name Damascus appears in the record of his achievements inscribed in the temple of Amun at Karnak: it is one of the places which he claims to have conquered. In the following century Damascus figures in the Amarna letters (the archives of the Egyptian foreign office under the 'heretic king' Akhnaton, 1369-1353 B.C.). The Amorite ruler of Damascus appears to have led a concerted attempt to throw off Egyptian domination, and Pharaoh's viceroy in that region had to enlist mercenaries from the Habiru to maintain control. (The term Habiru is probably the same as the biblical 'Hebrew'; Abraham himself is called 'the Hebrew' in Gen. 14.13.)

After the Amarna age Egyptian influence waned, and the Hittites began again to push southwards. Rameses II (1290-1224 B.C.) tried to establish Egyptian sovereignty again in Syria: after an inconclusive clash with the Hittites, he and the Hittite king reached an agreement (1270 B.C.) recognizing the river Orontes as the frontier of their empires, so that Damascus remained within the Egyptian sphere of influence.

About 1200 B.C. the fall of the Hittite Empire and the recession of Egyptian power laid that part of Syria open to invasion by the Aramaeans (a Semitic-speaking people from the desert), and it is as an Aramaean city that Damascus is thenceforth known in the Old Testament. Throughout the duration of the Israelite monarchy, from the time of David onwards (2 Sam. 8.5,6), the Aramaean kingdom of Damascus was a force to be reckoned with. The two kingdoms were usually at war with each other, except for brief occasions when the Assyrian threat from the east forced them to combine for common self-defence. Damascus first appears in Assyrian records in 853 B.C., when Shalmaneser III tells how Benhadad of Damascus (whom he calls Adad-'idri) and Ahab of Israel took part in a coalition which offered him resistance at Qarqar on the Orontes (this was during the three years' peace of 1 Kings 22.1). Damascus was finally conquered by the Assyrians in 732 B.C. (2 Kings 16.9) and became the centre of an Assyrian province.

Biblical references Genesis 15.2 – The status of Eliezer of Damascus as Abraham's heir was precarious. The spiritual inheritance involved in God's promise to Abraham rests on a surer foundation.

Acts 22.6-11 – Damascus figures only marginally in the story of Abraham. We may reflect, however, that the man who saw with unrivalled clarity what was involved for the world's salvation in God's promise to Abraham owed this insight to his confrontation near Damascus with the living Offspring of Abraham on whom the fulfilment of that promise depended.

Shechem

The modern city of Nablus stands near the site of biblical Shechem.

Shechem is the first place where Abraham is said to have halted after he entered Canaan from the north (Gen. 12.6). It was a city in the hill country of Ephraim (as that region was later called); its name, meaning 'shoulder' or 'saddle', was perhaps based on its position between Mount Ebal to the north and Mount Gerizim to the south. There God appeared to him, reaffirming and amplifying the promise he had already given him: 'To your descendants I will give this land' (Gen. 12.7). Abraham accordingly built an altar to the Lord there. There was no visible evidence that the divine promise was likely ever to be fulfilled; the land around was full of Canaanites. But the building of the altar bore witness to Abraham's faith in the promise and in him who gave it, while at the same time it was a token claiming of the land for Abraham's God. Abraham's action gave expression to a principle later embodied in the divine commandment of Exod. 20.24, that in every place where God should 'cause his name to be remembered' (i.e. should manifest his presence), his people should build 'an altar of earth' and worship him there.

It was natural that the place where the first altar was built in the promised land to the God of Abraham should be regarded as specially sacred. The 'oak (or terebinth) of Moreh' – or 'the diviner's oak' – beside which the altar stood, was a notable landmark for centuries to come (see Gen. 35.4; Josh. 24.26; Judges 9.37).

When Jacob, Abraham's grandson, returned to Canaan after his twenty years' sojourn in Haran, Shechem was the first place where he encamped on the west bank of the Jordan. He too built an altar there, in honour of El-Elohe-Israel ('El, the God of Israel'). He bought from the local inhabitants the land on which he encamped and shortly afterwards he and his family concluded a treaty with them. This treaty was treacherously broken by Simeon and Levi's attack on the Shechemites (Gen. 33.18-34.31). It was for this treacherous attack that, when Jacob on his deathbed pronounced a blessing on his sons, Simeon and Levi received a curse instead (Gen. 49.5-7).

When the Israelites returned from Egypt and the wilderness to settle in Canaan, they buried Joseph's bones, which they had brought with them, in the ground which Jacob had bought from the Shechemites and which he bequeathed to Joseph (Josh. 24.32). Nothing is said of the Israelites' conquering Shechem; archaeological evidence suggests that life continued undisturbed on the site during the period of the Israelite conquest of Canaan. It may be inferred, then, that there already existed a relationship or agreement between the Israelites and the Shechemites, going back to patriarchal times. The fact that worship was offered at Shechem to El-berith ('the God of the covenant') may bear witness to such an agreement (compare Judges 9.46). After the Israelite settlement, the blessings promised to the keepers of the law were recited on Mount Gerizim and the curses invoked on violators of the law on Mount Ebal, as Moses had commanded (Deut. 27.11-13; Josh. 8.30-35). It was at Shechem,

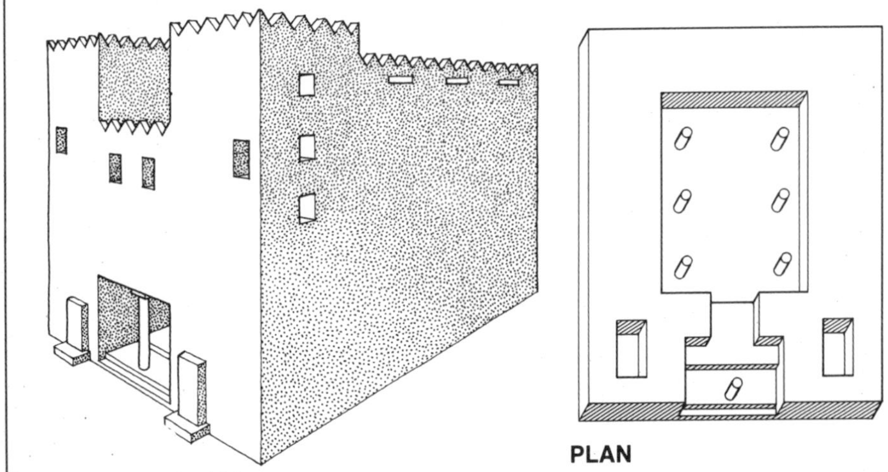

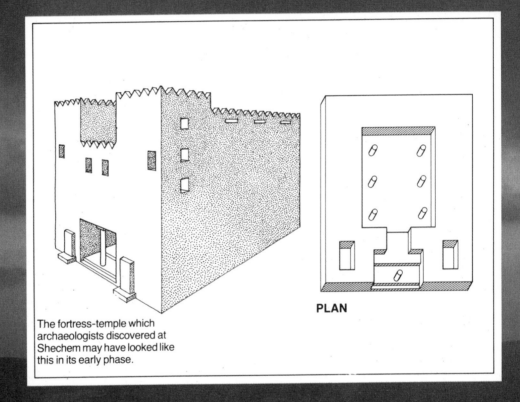

The fortress-temple which archaeologists discovered at Shechem may have looked like this in its early phase.

too, that Joshua mustered the tribes of Israel so that they might renew their covenant with the God of their fathers. A 'great stone' was set up under the terebinth 'in the sanctuary of the Lord' to commemorate the occasion (Josh. 24.25-27).

The curious story of Abimelech, son of Gideon, tells of the hostility which, at a later date, broke out between the Israelites and the Shechemites and led to the destruction of Shechem (Judges 9.1-49).

When the Israelite monarchy fell apart after Solomon's death (about 930 B.C.), Jeroboam, leader of the revolt against Solomon's son, rebuilt Shechem and made it the capital of the northern kingdom (1 Kings 12.25); it did not retain this status for long, for it was soon replaced by Tirzah.

Shechem, because of its ancient associations with Abraham and other patriarchs, has been treated for well over 2,000 years by the Samaritans as the holiest spot on earth, the place chosen by God for his dwelling (Deut. 12.5). When the Samaritan woman said to Jesus, 'Our fathers worshipped on this mountain' (John 4.20), it was to Mount

Samaritan remains on the summit of Mount Gerizim, near biblical Shechem.

Gerizim that she pointed: on it the Samaritans had a temple from about 400 to 108 B.C.

The site of ancient Shechem is identified with Tell-Balatah, a mile or two east of the modern city of Nablus. The name Nablus preserves the Greek Neapolis ('new city'); Flavia Neapolis was the name of a city which the Emperor Vespasian founded there in A.D. 72.

One of the earliest references to the place in written records comes in an inscription of the Egyptian king Sesostris III (1878-1843 B.C.), not long after Abraham's time. He tells how, during an invasion of Canaan, he reduced Sekmem, which was evidently a fortified city-state. Shechem was occupied by the Egyptians again after the expulsion of the Hyksos invaders (1570 B.C.). It figures in the Amarna correspondence (about 1360 B.C.) as a centre of anti-Egyptian intrigue; its rulers are accused of making common cause with the Habiru invaders. It has been conjectured that this could be a reference to the agreement bet-

Inset: Part of the site of ancient Shechem (Tell Balatah) has been excavated by archaeologists.

Mount Gerizim as seen from the slopes of Mount Ebal.

ween the sons of Jacob and the Shechemites (Gen. 34.8-24); this is quite doubtful.

The site has been excavated at various times in the twentieth century – by German archaeologists before and after World War I, and by an American expedition under G. E. Wright and others from 1956 to 1973. As a result of these excavations, it is possible to distinguish successive phases of the occupation of Shechem; in the Middle Bronze Age, ending with the Egyptian conquest after the expulsion of the Hyksos; in the Late Bronze Age, from about 1450 B.C. to the destruction of the city about 1125 B.C. (presumably that recorded in the story of Abimelech); in the Iron Age (under the Israelite monarchy until the Assyrian conquest of 732 B.C.); and then from about 330 to 108 B.C. a Hellenistic city associated with the Samaritan temple on Mount Gerizim. Temple and city alike were destroyed by the Jewish king John Hyrcanus; but what is possibly the base of the altar of that temple, on a side of 65 feet and with a

Inset: The ancient city wall at Tell Balatah.

Tell Balatah, the site of biblical Shechem.

height of 32 feet, survives on Tell er-Ras, on the northern peak of Gerizim.

The principal remains uncovered by archaeology are the two great city gates and the Cyclopean city wall of the Hyksos period (about 1600 B.C.) and the succession of temples at the west end of the city, each succeeding one being built on top of its predecessors, regardless of political changes. The temple which stood here during the Late Bronze Age may well have been the temple of El-berith or Baal-berith mentioned in Judges 9.4,46. Other ancient shrines have been identified on Tell Balatah, providing further testimony to its sacred associations in antiquity.

Biblical references Genesis 12.6 – On entering the promised land Abraham stopped at Shechem and built his first altar there. If this was a token claiming of the land for God, what kind of action would serve as a similar token today? No further visit by Abraham to Shechem is recorded, but this first visit set an indelible stamp on the place. It is noteworthy that only a little way to the east of Shechem, many centuries after Abraham's day, Jesus, the Son of Abraham (Matt. 1.1), taught a daughter of Abraham how the true God, who is pure Spirit, should be worshipped 'in spirit and truth' (John 4.23,24).

Bethel

Bethel is first mentioned in the Bible in Gen. 12.8 where Abraham, after leaving Shechem, is said to have 'removed to the mountain on the east of Bethel, and pitched his tent, with Bethel on the west and Ai on the east'. As at Shechem, so here too he built an altar to the Lord and worshipped him by name. From Bethel he struck camp and journeyed south into the Negeb, and then on into Egypt. On his return from Egypt 'he journeyed on from the Negeb as far as Bethel, to the place where his tent had been at the beginning, between Bethel and Ai, to the place where he had made an altar at the first' (Gen. 13.3,4), and there again he invoked the Lord by name. It was here, apparently, that he and Lot agreed to go their separate ways because the surrounding countryside was not adequate to support the flocks and herds of both of them.

Bethel is commonly identified with the

A barren landscape near Et Tell, the probable location of biblical Ai, the city which lay east of Bethel.

A bedouin leads his camels through Sinai.

modern village of Beitin, lying 2,886 feet above sea level, between ten and eleven miles north of Jerusalem. It has no natural defences but is well watered by springs and stands at the point where the north-south mountain road crosses the east-west road from Jericho to the Mediterranean. The strategic importance of the place is recognized today: nearby is the military settlement from which the Israeli authorities control the whole of the occupied west bank of Palestine and for which, indeed, they have taken over the name Bethel. The 'mountain on the east of Bethel', where Abraham encamped, is probably El-Burj, less than half a mile ESE of Beitin. From here one can easily command, in Dean Stanley's words, a 'survey of the country . . . such as can be enjoyed from no other point in the neighbourhood'. It was from such a vantage-point that Lot 'saw that the Jordan valley was well watered everywhere

A typical bedouin encampment in barren desert country. The tents are surrounded by the bedouin flocks and herds.

like the garden of the Lord' (Gen. 13.10), and chose it as his residence.

Ai can be identified with no other site in the neighbourhood than the impressive and thoroughly excavated ruin of Et-Tell, about a mile and a half ESE of Bethel. The work Ai means 'ruin'. The city had been destroyed towards the end of the Early Bronze Age (about 2300 B.C.) and lay derelict for many centuries; it was already a 'ruin' when Abraham encamped between Bethel and Ai.

The site of Bethel was excavated in 1934 and later in 1954, 1957 and 1960. In 1960 a hilltop sanctuary was discovered going back to the beginning of the Middle Bronze Age. It is from this time (not long before 2000 B.C.) that the continuous occupation of the site is to be dated. We should therefore envisage some kind of city there when Abraham pitched his tent nearby, but it was not until later (between about 1750 and 1650 B.C.) that the entire area was surrounded by a strong wall. This was early in the Hyksos period; indeed, two phases of fortification, with some evidence of destruction separating them, have been distinguished in this period. The second of these phases was completed not long before the Egyptians expelled the Hyksos from their own land and pursued them into Canaan, destroying Bethel on their way. After a century or two it was restored: it was this Late Bronze Age city that the Israelites captured about 1200 B.C. (Josh. 10.16; Judges 1.22-25). For the rest of the biblical narrative Bethel appears as an Israelite city.

But Bethel figures most memorably in the biblical narrative back in the patriarchal period, in the life-story of Jacob, Abraham's grandson. It was at Bethel that Jacob spent the first night of his journey from Beer-sheba to Haran, when he fled from the vengeance of his brother Esau; it was there that he saw in his dream the ladder reaching up to heaven and received the promise of God that the land on which he lay would be his and that he would have a multitude of descendants to populate it (Gen. 28.10-22). When he awoke, Jacob recognized that God must have his dwelling there, so he set up a commemorative pillar and poured a libation of olive oil on it to consecrate it. The name of the place was thenceforth Bethel, 'the house of God'; its Canaanite name had been Luz (Gen. 18.19; Judges 1.23,26). On his return from Haran, twenty years later, Jacob revisited the place and built an altar there to El-bethel ('the God of Bethel'), and God reconfirmed his earlier promises to him (Gen. 35.6-15). The memory of his encounter with God at Bethel remained with Jacob to the end of his days: when Joseph brought his two sons to receive his father's deathbed blessing, the old man began by recalling how 'God Almighty appeared to me at Luz in the land of Canaan and blessed me' (Gen. 48.3).

At the time of the Israelite settlement in Canaan, Bethel was assigned to the tribe of Benjamin (Josh. 18.13), but it was evidently retaken by the Canaanites (as indeed the archaeological record suggests), from whom it was captured by members of the family of Joseph (Judges 1.22-25). From then on it was reckoned to the territory of Ephraim. The ark of the covenant was housed at Bethel for some years in the period of the judges, under the priesthood of Phinehas, Aaron's grandson (Judges 20.26-28). When the kingdom was divided after Solomon's death, Bethel lay near the southern frontier of the northern kingdom of Israel. Accordingly, King Jeroboam made the ancient sanctuary there one of the

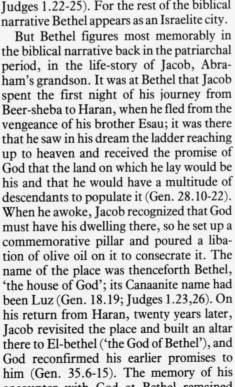

Remains of the city wall at Et Tell, which is probably to be identified with Ai, the city the Israelites captured after the fall of Jericho. Excavations have revealed a city which prospered in the 3rd millennium BC.

two official shrines of his kingdom (the other being that at Dan, in the far north), as a rival to Jerusalem, which belonged to the southern kingdom of Judah. There he set up one of the two golden bull-calves to serve as the pedestal of the invisible presence of the God of Israel (1 Kings 12.26-33).

It was at Bethel, during one of the great national festivals, that the prophet Amos delivered his public protests and warnings until Amaziah, the priest of Bethel, ordered him home to Judah (Amos 7.10-17). After the Assyrian conquest of the land, which Amos had foretold, the sanctuary at Bethel remained in being, for it was a priest of Bethel who taught the law of the God of Israel to the immigrants whom the Assyrian kings forcibly settled in Samaria from other parts of their empire (2 Kings 17.28). But exactly a hundred years after the Assyrian conquest, the sanctuary at Bethel was desecrated and demolished in 621 B.C. by Josiah, king of Judah, during his campaign

Beitin, about twelve miles north of Jerusalem, is the probable site of biblical Bethel.

Another view of the impressive remains at Et Tell (Ai).

to abolish the 'high places' and centralize priesthood and sacrifice at Jerusalem (2 Kings 23.15-18).

After the return from the Babylonian exile Bethel was reoccupied by a small Jewish community (Ezra 2.28; Neh. 7.32), which increased substantially as time went on.

Biblical references Gen. 12.8 – Jacob discovered that the Lord was at Bethel, although he had not known this. Abraham's action at Bethel was much less spectacular; he pitched his tent there, built an altar and 'called on the name of the Lord'. Perhaps he already knew the truth expressed by one of our own hymn-writers:

Where'er they seek thee, thou art found,
And every place is hallowed ground.

Gen. 13.3-17 – We have no right to condemn Lot for the choice which he made at Bethel, when he decided to settle in the plain of Jordan. Abraham had encouraged him to make the prior choice, and Lot could not possibly have foreseen the disaster which would overtake Sodom and the neighbouring cities. What stands out in the narrative is Abraham's faith, his readiness to leave his own interests in the hand of God.

The view from El Burj south-east towards Ai.

Egypt

This reproduction of the wall-painting from the tomb of Menna in Egypt represents Egyptian harvest scenes.

After leaving Bethel Abraham continued his journey south into the Negeb, and from there he 'went down' into Egypt because of a famine (Gen. 12.10). This is the first occasion on which the land of Egypt is mentioned in the biblical narrative. Abraham's temporary descent into Egypt because of famine anticipates the descent on a much larger scale and for a much longer sojourn undertaken by his descendants three or four generations later, in the days of Jacob and Joseph (Gen. 42.1-47.28).

It was a very natural thing to go to Egypt when Syria and Palestine were hit by famine. Syria and Palestine depended for their fertility on regular rainfall: when for any reason the rain failed, even for one season (let alone for several), the crops could not grow and there was nothing for human beings or domestic animals to eat. But Egypt was governed by a quite different weather system: very little rain ever fell in Egypt, but so long as the Nile rose year by year and flooded the adjoining land, leaving a fresh deposit of fertile mud, Egypt could be sure of abundant crops. The rise of the Nile began in June and reached its peak in September, and the flood-waters were carefully guided by canals and ditches to the areas where they were required. (This seasonal rhythm has now been quite changed by the perennial irrigation system controlled by the dams at Aswan and elsewhere.)

The Israelites, in their wilderness wanderings of later days, looked back to the time in Egypt when they 'sat by the flesh-pots and ate bread to the full' (Exod. 16.3), when fish could be eaten for nothing because they were so plentiful and they enjoyed 'the cucumbers, the melons, the leeks, the onions, and the garlic' (Num. 11.5). The same fertility in the Delta and in the narrow cultivated strip along both banks of the Nile can be appreciated today: those parts of Egypt are still, as they were then, 'like a garden of vegetables' (Deut. 11.10). True, even Egypt could experience famine (as it did for seven years in Joseph's day) if the Nile did not rise high enough; but the

The great Sphinx and the Chefren Pyramid at Gaza, Egypt, where the greatest of all the pyramids were built.

conditions which prevented the Nile from rising were different from those which caused the failure of rainfall in Syria and Palestine, so that famine in Syria and Palestine would rarely coincide with scarcity in Egypt.

Ancient Egypt comprised two main areas, which were originally separate kingdoms: the northern kingdom (Lower Egypt), consisting of the Nile delta, and the southern kingdom (Upper Egypt), comprising the strip of fertile territory on either side of the Nile from the region of modern Cairo up to the first cataract, at Aswan. The historical dynasties of Egype are numbered from the unification of the two kingdoms about 3000 B.C. The cultural and political highpoints of ancient Egyptian history were reached during the Old Kingdom or pyramid age (Dynasties III-VI, about 2560-2200 B.C.), the Middle Kingdom (Dynasties XI-XII, about 2134-1786 B.C.) and the New Kingdom (Dynasties XVIII-XX, about 1570-1085 B.C.). The buildings, carvings,

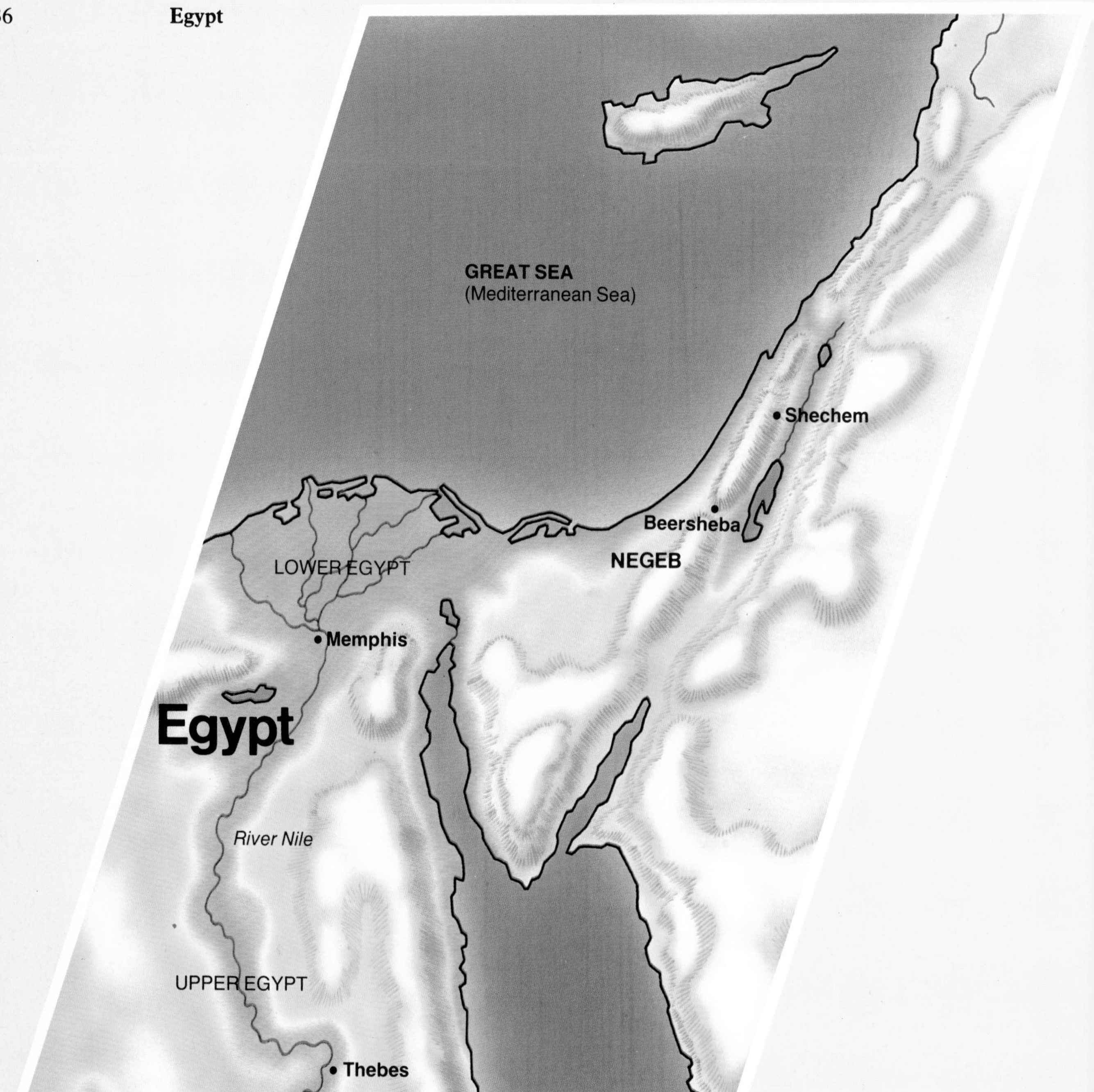

paintings and written records of those periods of cultural achievement provide us with an abundance of historical information about them.

Abraham's descent to Egypt is well illustrated by a painting on the walls of the rock-tomb of a local governor named Khnum-hotep, on the east bank of the Nile, at Beni Hassan in Middle Egypt, to be dated shortly after 1900 B.C. The painting depicts a party of nomads from Asia, led by a man who is called a 'desert chieftain', who is accompanied by women and children. The Asians are described as bringing black eye-paint from the land of Shut (perhaps the Sheth of Num. 24.17), probably located in Transjordan. They seem to have been wandering tinkers and musicians, to judge by a pair of bellows and a lyre which are transported on the backs of two greyish-brown donkeys. There is no reason at all to identify this particular migration with Abraham's descent, but it presents an example of the kind of peaceful penetration which was constantly taking place.

A less peaceful penetration from Asia was

the invasion of the Hyksos (the 'chiefs of foreign lands') who established themselves in the north-eastern Delta about 1720 B.C. and extended their power over the country for nearly 150 years. The Hyksos ascendancy took place substantially later than Abraham's time; it does, however, provide an acceptable setting for the story of Joseph. The expulsion of the Hyksos was followed by the New Kingdom of Dynasties XVIII-XX. The kings of the eighteenth dynasty not only expelled the Hyksos from Egypt but pursued them into Palestine and Syria, destroying a number of their strongholds. The most powerful ruler of this dynasty, Thothmes III (1490-1436 B.C.), carried his arms as far north as the Euphrates. The nineteenth dynasty (about 1300-1200 B.C.) is most commonly thought to have been that during which the Israelites' deliverance from Egyptian bondage under Moses took place. Rameses II, the most outstanding king of this dynasty, is generally identified with the Pharaoh of the oppression. His long reign of sixty-seven years (about 1290-1224 B.C.) is commemorated by great buildings in all parts of Egypt and by numerous gigantic reproductions of his own likeness in stone, many of them now fragmentary (like the one celebrated in Shelley's *Ozymandias*). One of the best preserved of his statues now dominates Rameses Square in Cairo, outside the railway station. The great military event of his

A papyrus sheet from ancient Egypt illustrating agricultural scenes, including ploughing. Papyrus reed stems were used to make mats, baskets, furniture, sandals, boats and roofs of houses as well as paper.

This Egyptian tomb-painting shows a smith from Palestine.

reign was his battle with the king of the Hittites at Kadesh on the Orontes, in Syria (about 1286 B.C.). It was not the overwhelming victory that Rameses claims on his monuments: the result was rather stalemate, as the two kings acknowledged in a treaty several years later, which fixed the Orontes as the boundary between their two empires.

The kings of Egypt continued to play a part in biblical history, off and on, down to the Babylonian exile. Solomon's queen was a daughter of one of the kings of Dynasty XXI (about 960 B.C.). The founder of the next dynasty, Shishak, took a different line: he encouraged Jeroboam and others to rebel against Solomon (1 Kings 11.40) and some years later he raided the land of Israel (1 Kings 14.25-28), as he himself records in a relief-scene in the temple of Amun at Karnak (about 918 B.C.). Later kings of Egypt tried to use the kings of Israel and Judah to pull their chestnuts out of the fire by rebelling against their Assyrian and Babylonian overlords (2 Kings 17.4; Ezek. 17.11-17), but gave them no help against the overlords' reprisals. The beginning of the end for the kingdom of Judah was good King Josiah's fatal attempt in 608 B.C. to deny passage to Pharaoh Neco when he marched into Asia to try to shore up the collapsing Assyrian Empire (2 Kings 23:29). But if Josiah could not bar Neco's advance, Nebuchadnezzar did so three

Wind-swept sand dunes in the Negeb Desert.

Inset: Tomb-painting from ancient Egypt showing Egyptian girls, one of whom is playing the pipes. Their distinctive hairstyle and fine clothing mark them out as privileged Egyptians.

years later, at Carchemish on the Euphrates, and drove him back into Egypt (Jer. 46.2).

If Abraham is rightly dated early in the Middle Bronze Age (about 1900 B.C.), then Dynasty XII was in power when he visited Egypt. The kings of this dynasty found Thebes in Upper Egypt (modern Luxor), where the preceding dynasty had ruled, too far south for the convenient control of the whole country; they therefore moved their capital to Ithet Tawy, near Memphis (about twelve miles south of Cairo), on the west bank of the Nile. It was here, no doubt, that Abraham was admitted to the presence of Pharaoh (perhaps Amenemhet II, 1929-1865 B.C.). Had the court been at Thebes, as it was immediately before and immediately after Dynasty XII, Pharaoh's attention might not have been drawn so readily to these temporary visitors. Abraham nearly got himself and Pharaoh into trouble by representing Sarah to be his sister, not his wife – a practice of which more will be said in the section on Gerar (page 47). But the upshot was that Abraham left Egypt richer than when he came, thanks to the gifts which Pharaoh bestowed on him.

About 1960 B.C., under the previous king, an Egyptian named Sinuhe escaped to Asia, eluding the frontier guards, and arrived at Qedem in Transjordan, where he remained for eighteen months. After various adventures, related in his own words, he returned to Egypt and made his peace with Pharaoh.

Inset: Rameses II of Egypt, who was responsible for building the great temple of Abu Simbel. He was possibly pharaoh at the time when the Israelites fled from Egypt under the leadership of Moses.

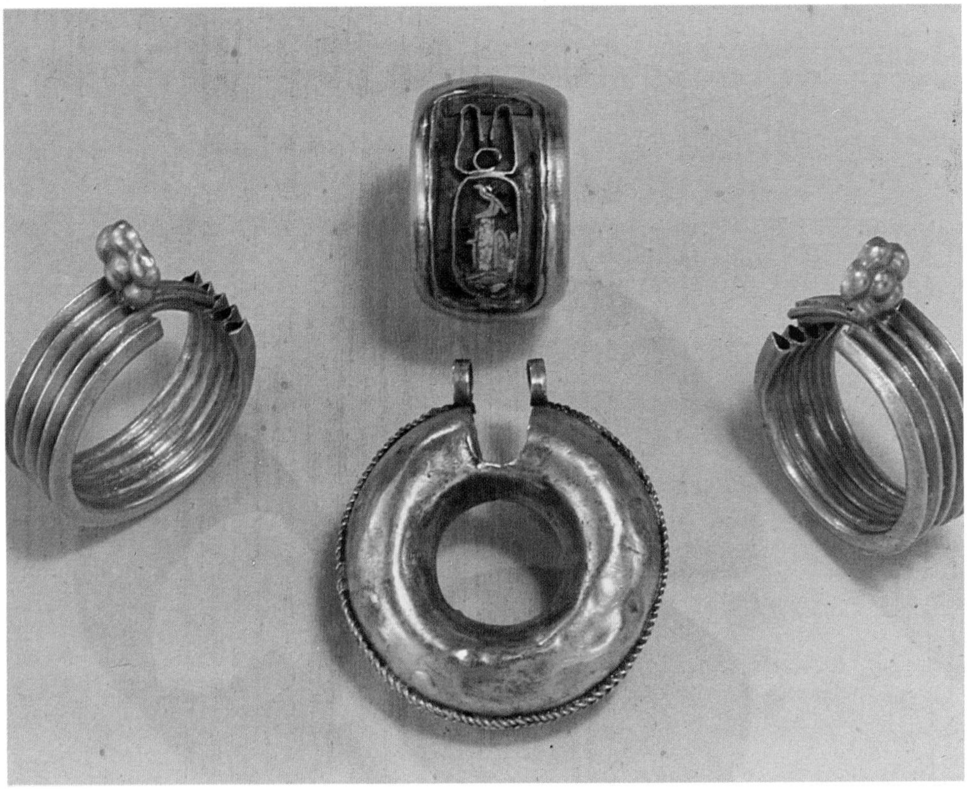

These gold earrings date from the New Kingdom period in Egyptian history, c 1500–1200 BC.

A model funeral boat, like those used to carry the coffins of wealthy Egyptians to their tombs.

Pharaoh (Sesostris I, 1971-1928 B.C.) gave the same kind of orders for the protection of the returning Sinuhe as his successor gave for the departing Abraham.

Biblical references Gen. 12.10-20 – The Bible has nothing more to say of Abraham's association with Egypt beyond what is contained in these twenty verses. There is an allegorical school of biblical interpretation which treats Egypt as a symbol of the godless world, and therefore looks on Abraham's visit to Egypt as self-evidently deplorable, almost as though his 'going down' there implies that he went down in a moral sense. (But 'going down to Egypt' is a regular geographical expression in Old and New Testaments.) Do you think this is right? Does the fact that it was a famine that made him go down imply a lack of faith on his part? (There is no suggestion to this effect in the narrative itself.) A little later in Abraham's career he refused to give the king of Sodom the opportunity of enriching him (Gen. 14.21-23); yet here he does not refuse to accept the wealth which Pharaoh lavishes on him. Does this call for comment? His half-truth about his wife certainly calls for comment, but this will come up for consideration later (page 47).

Mamre

After Lot parted company with Abraham, to take up residence in the lower Jordan valley, Abraham 'moved his tent, and came and dwelt by the oaks (or terebinths) of Mamre, which are at Hebron; and there he built an altar to the Lord' (Gen. 13.18).

The site of Mamre is known to the Arabs today as Ramat el-Halil, 'the high place of the Friend' (i.e. Abraham, the Friend of God). Hebron itself is known to them as El-Halil, 'the Friend', because of Abraham's association with it, but Hebron's existence as a city began some 200 years after Abraham's day (see Num. 13.22). The name Hebron means 'confederation'; the city was evidently formed by the union of four distinct settlements, as is indicated by its old name Kiriath-arba, 'city of four' (Gen. 23.2). Mamre is about $1^2/_3$ miles north of Hebron, 3,250 feet above sea level.

In so far as Abraham had a place in Canaan which could be called his home, it

A tree at Mamre. Abraham lived for considerable periods under the terebinth of Mamre, and built an altar there.

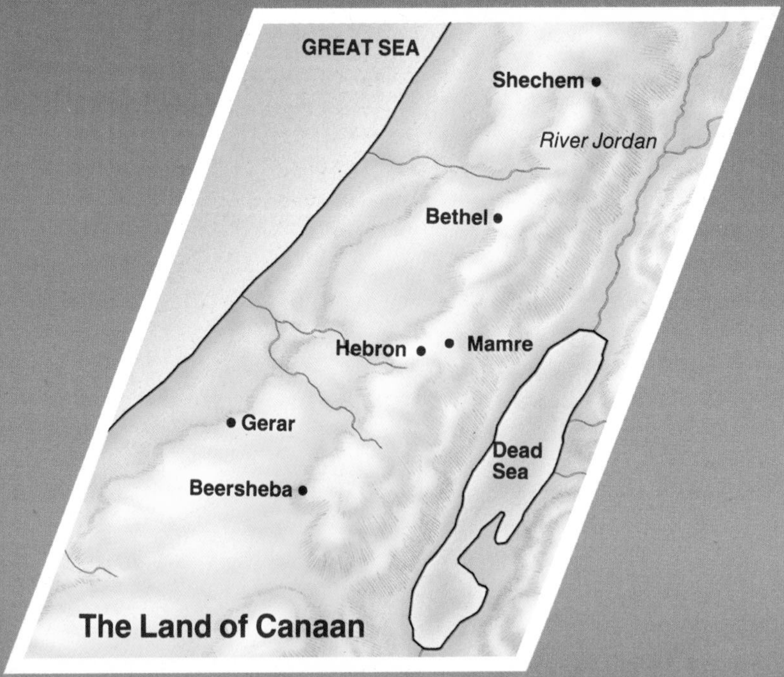

Ramet el-Khalil, the modern name for biblical Mamre, is about two miles north of Hebron.

was at Mamre. His family and household could stay here while he was leading caravans or taking part in pastoral activity elsewhere. It was at Mamre that he and Sarah 'entertained angels unawares' (Gen. 18.1-15); that was the occasion on which they received the promise of God that within a year Sarah, against all natural expectation, would give birth to a son. That was the occasion, too, on which Abraham pleaded with God to spare the city of Sodom, and God undertook to spare it if but ten righteous men could be found there (Gen. 18.16-33). In the event, not even ten righteous men were found, and from the spot where Abraham had pleaded with God he saw the smoke of Sodom and its neighbouring cities rising high in the air (Gen. 19.27,28).

Many years later, when Jacob returned from his twenty years exile in Mesopotamia, it was at Mamre that he visited his aged father Isaac (Gen. 35.27).

There is a group of ancient buildings there, known locally as Beit el-Halil, 'house of the Friend'. These were excavated from 1926 to 1928 by a German archaeological expedition under the direction of Evaristus Mader. Here, it was established, was the site of a basilica built by the Emperor Constantine (about A.D. 330) in the vicinity of a huge terebinth tree which was believed to be the one under which Abraham had built his altar. (Two and a half centuries before Constantine, the Jewish historian Josephus described the terebinth: it was believed, he says, that it had survived there from patriarchal times.) The archaeological expedition also established that Constantine's basilica was built on the site of an earlier holy place. The church historian Sozomen, who lived in the fifth century A.D., has preserved a description of the place before Constantine built his church. There was a stone enclosure there within which a religious fair was held every summer. Pagans, Jews and Christians came from

Inset: A view from the site of Mamre.

Inside the walled enclosure dating from Herodian times at Mamre, near Hebron.

near and far: Jews and Christians prayed to the God of Abraham, while the pagans worshipped their own deities. The well within the sacred enclosure (held, naturally, to be that from which Abraham's household drew water when they stayed at Mamre) was now regarded as too holy for common use: it was treated as a wishing well, into which pilgrims threw coins, incense and other precious things, and by the side of which they lit lamps.

Constantine's mother-in-law visited the place once during the fair, and was so shocked by the pagan rites and the hilarity with which they were conducted that she complained to the emperor. He put a stop to the pagan practices, destroyed the existing altar and images, and built his basilica on the site. The basilica occupied the eastern half of the enclosure; the western half served as a forecourt, containing the well and the terebinth.

The character of the masonry of the enclosure shows it to have been the work of Herod the Great, like the enclosure at Machpelah, not far away (see p. 57). The site would be specially revered by Herod, since he was not only a Jew by religion but an Idumaean (Edomite) by birth, and thus descended from Abraham through his grandson Esau. Herod's building suffered serious damage in the Jewish revolt against Rome which broke out in A.D. 66, but it was restored, with the same Herodian stones, by the Emperor Hadrian, when he had put down a second Jewish revolt in A.D. 135. At that time Hadrian offered the defeated Jews as great an insult as could be imagined when he turned the sacred enclosure into a Gentile market-place where his Jewish captives were sold as slaves.

Long before Herod's time, however, Mamre appears to have been venerated as a sanctuary. Under the kings of Judah a paved 'sacred way' led to it from the main Jerusalem – Hebron road; but pottery found on the site indicates that it was frequented in the Early Bronze Age (third millennium B.C.), well before Abraham's time.

An anonymous pilgrim from Bordeaux, who left a record of a visit which he paid to the Holy Land in A.D. 333, describes the place, which he calls Terebinthus: here, he says, 'Abraham lived and dug a well beneath the terebinth tree, and talked and ate with angels; an exceptionally beautiful basilica has been built there by command of Constantine.' The terebinth was evidently still to be seen in A.D. 333; it perished soon afterwards, during the reign of Constantius (A.D. 337-361). But the place continued to be known by the name of the tree even after the tree disappeared; it is marked as Terebinthos on the Medeba map (a mosaic map of the Holy Land constructed in the floor of a Byzantine church at Medeba, in Transjordan, between A.D. 560 and 565). Even after Constantine's attempt to purify the site, pagan rites persisted there, as Eusebius and Jerome assure us: 'the place of the terebinth is frequented superstitiously

The wall of Herod's enclosure, Mamre. Later the Emperor Constantine built a basilica beside an ancient terebinth known as the tree beneath which Abraham 'entertained angels unawares'.

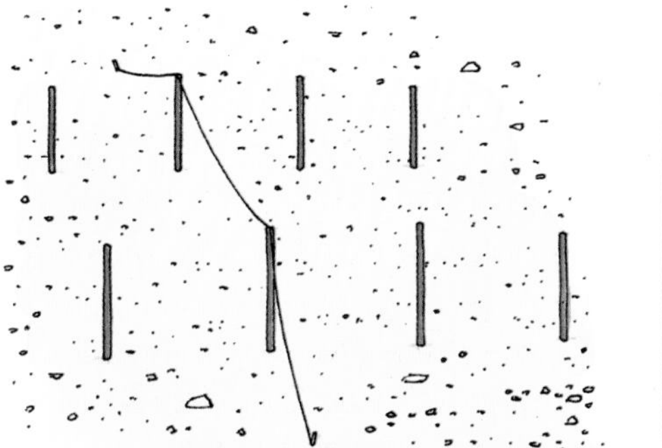

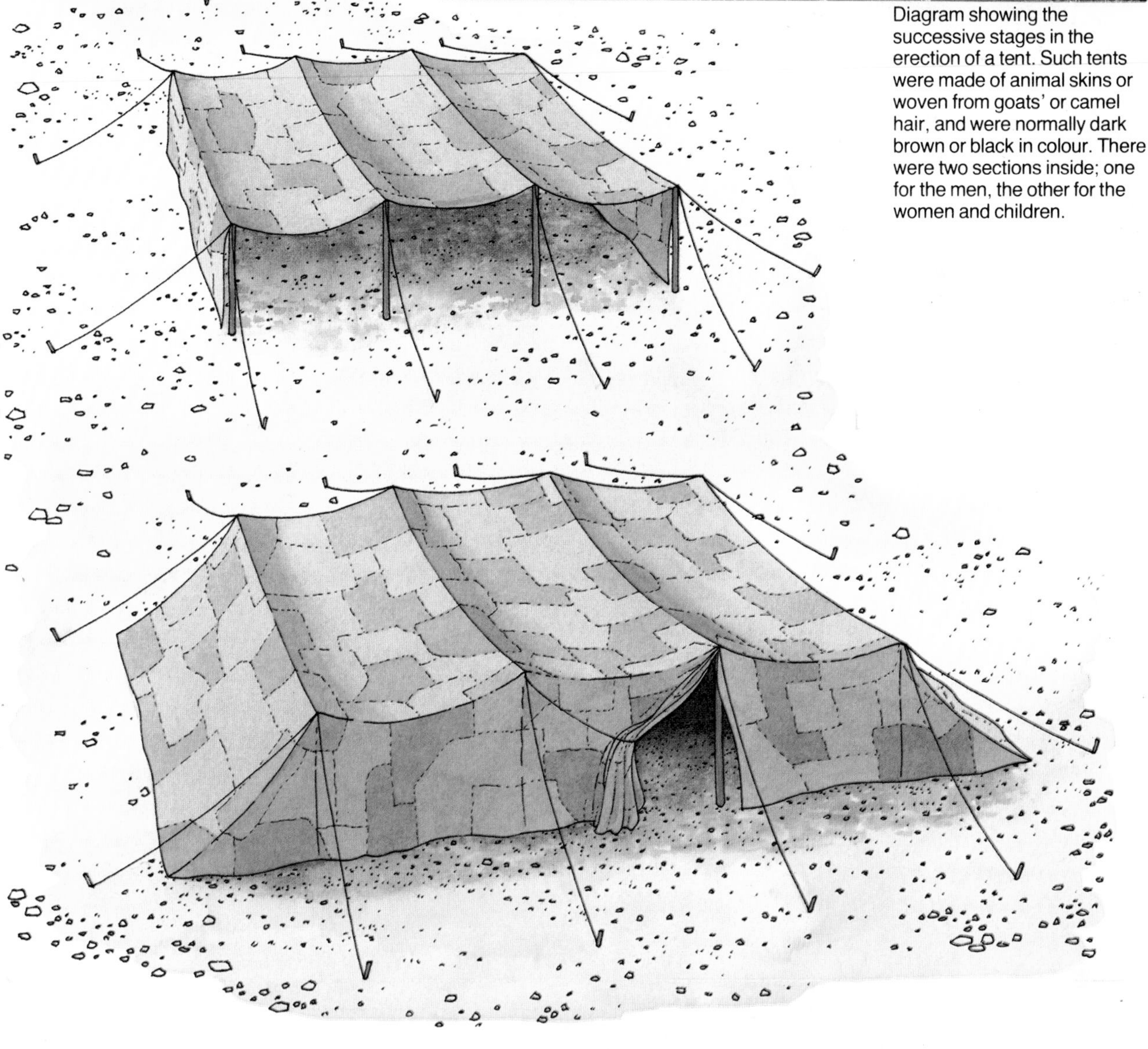

Diagram showing the successive stages in the erection of a tent. Such tents were made of animal skins or woven from goats' or camel hair, and were normally dark brown or black in colour. There were two sections inside; one for the men, the other for the women and children.

Sodom, one of the cities of the plain, was probably located in the great rift valley, near the Dead Sea.

by all the surrounding ethnic groups.' To Jews, Christians and Muslims, however, its fame is based on the fact that it was here that Abraham stayed and had those dealings with God which have won for him the name 'The Friend of God'.

Biblical references Gen. 18.1-33 – Of all Abraham's experiences at Mamre, the visitation recorded in this chapter is outstanding. In the New Testament the occasion is made the subject of an exhortation: 'Do not neglect to show hospitality to strangers, for thereby some have entertained angels unawares' (Heb. 13.2). And indeed, the picture it gives of spontaneous hospitality is unforgettable. There is quiet humour, too, in Sarah's incredulous laughter, natural enough at her age, at the announcement that she would have a son. But the two features that specially stand out are God's tribute to Abraham – 'Shall I hide from Abraham what I am about to do . . .?' (v. 17) – and Abraham's intercession with God for the wicked city of Sodom (vs. 22-33). One gets the impression that if Abraham had gone on to plead that the city might be spared if only five righteous men were found there, God would still have given him a positive response. As it was, Sodom was not spared but Abraham's prayer did not go completely unanswered: 'God remembered Abraham, and sent Lot out of the midst of the overthrow, when he overthrew the cities in which Lot dwelt' (Gen 19.29).

Gerar

Gerar was a place in the Negeb where Abraham took up residence for a period after the destruction of Sodom (Gen. 20.1). It is identified with Tell Abu Hureirah, on the main road from Gaza to Beer-sheba, about fifteen miles from the former and twelve miles from the latter. It lay near the Egyptian frontier of Canaan, and was a leading caravan centre.

Gerar, in Abraham's time, was a royal city, the residence of a king bearing the Canaanite name Abimelech. Abimelech's territory appears to have included Beer-sheba (Gen. 21.22-32).

When Abraham settled in Gerar he adopted his regular policy and introduced Sarah as his sister. (He had already done this, with awkward results, in Egypt.) In Haran, from which they had come to Canaan, she was legally his sister before she became his wife, and did not lose the former status on acquiring the latter. Isaac similarly introduced Rebekah as his sister (Gen. 26.7), for she was related to him by blood on his father's side. Jacob, on the other hand, does not speak of Leah and Rachel as his sisters, for his blood-relationship with them was through his mother. But through concealing the fact that Sarah was his wife as well as his sister, Abraham exposed her to a risk which might have put in question the legitimacy of Isaac, so soon to be born to them. When Abimelech, who had accommodated her in his harem, discovered that she was Abraham's wife, he remonstrated with Abraham, not without justification, for putting him in a situation where he might unwittingly have committed a serious sin. After the misunderstanding was cleared up, Abimelech treated Abraham generously, giving him a monetary recompense for the injury inadvertently done to him, and inviting him to settle in whatever part of his territory he pleased.

Isaac, a generation later, also settled in Gerar with his wife Rebekah and his retain-

This Egyptian wall-painting shows Pharaoh Rameses II, who was possibly Pharaoh at the time of the Exodus, conquering Nubia.

ers and flocks, in a time of famine, and had dealings with another Abimelech (Gen. 26.1-16). He became so wealthy and powerful there that Abimelech at last begged him to leave, so Isaac encamped in the valley of Gerar – best identified with the deep Wadi Esh-Shari'ah, south and east of Tell Abu Hureirah.

Tell Abu Hureirah is one of the largest tells in the region: the site was occupied as far back as the Chalcolithic and Early

Camels take a well-earned rest in Sinai.

Bronze Ages (between 3500 and 3000 B.C.). There is a special abundance of potsherds from that part of the Middle Bronze Age which is commonly equated with the age of the patriarchs. The city stretched from the summit of the tell to the south and east towards the Wadi esh-Shari'ah, covering an area of between 35 and 40 acres. At this time it seems to have the largest and most powerful city in the Negeb. Beer-sheba, which was to occupy that distinction under the monarchy, does not appear to have been a city at all in patriarchal times.

Gerar does not figure in the accounts of the distribution of the land of Canaan among the tribes of Israel. About the same time as the Israelites were penetrating the Negeb from the landward side, the Philistines landed on the coastal plain and pressed inland, occupying Gerar for some generations. This is probably why in Gen. 26.1-18 the people of Gerar are called

A shepherd with his flock at sunset in the Negeb.

The barren landscape of the Negeb.

A view near Tell Gerar, probable site of biblical Gerar, where both Abraham and Isaac stayed.

Abraham and Isaac dug wells at Gerar, located in the foothills of the Judean mountains.

Philistines – e.g., they are given the name of the people who subsequently occupied the district.

According to the early Greek version of the Old Testament, members of the tribe of Simeon, at a later date, in the reign of Hezekiah (about 700 B.C.), trekked 'to the entrance of Gerar, to the east side of the valley, to seek pasture for their flocks, where they found rich, good pasture, and the land was very broad, quiet, and peaceful; for the former inhabitants there belonged to Ham' (1 Chron. 4.39,40 where the Hebrew text has the otherwise unknown place-name Gedor). The reference to Ham may denote the Canaanite origin of the earlier inhabitants, since Canaan was a son of Ham (Gen. 9.22; 10.6), or it may point to their association with Egypt (called 'the land of Ham' in Psa. 105.23). The Simeonites dispossessed the earlier population and settled there themselves.

The last appearance of Gerar in the biblical narrative is as the centre of the district where Asa, king of Judah (910-870 B.C.), routed an army of invading Ethiopians (i.e. Nubians) under their king Zerah (2 Chron. 14.13,14).

Biblical references Gen. 20.1-18 – It is not for us, who are imperfectly acquainted with the ideas of propriety which operated in the Near East in patriarchal times, to pass moral judgments on Abraham's behaviour. But what did the narrator think? Does he imply that Abraham was in the wrong in concealing an important part of the truth from Abimelech – as earlier from Pharaoh (Gen. 12.11-20)? On the one hand, he engages the reader's sympathy with Abimelech, who acted in innocence; on the other hand, he represents Abraham as an acceptable and effective intercessor with God on Abimelech's behalf. Does this suggest that Abraham had no consciousness of wrongdoing (compare Psa. 66.18)? Certainly in Gerar, as in Egypt, Abraham profited substantially from the misunderstanding.

Gen. 20.7 – God says of Abraham, 'he is a prophet'. What is the significance of this in the immediate context of the present story and in the wider context of the life of Abraham? Compare Psa. 105.12-15.

Bedouin women at the Arab market in modern Beersheba.

Beersheba

When Abimelech, king of Gerar, invited Abraham to settle in whatever part of his territory he chose, Abraham settled for a considerable time in the region of Beersheba. There he and Abimelech swore an oath and made a covenant (Gen. 21.22-32), and for this reason the place was called Beer-sheba ('the well of the oath'). The oath and the consequent naming of the place are repeated in the next generation in the story of Isaac (Gen. 26.31,32). An alternative explanation of the place-name ('the well of seven') may be implied in the incident of the seven ewe lambs which Abraham gave to Abimelech to witness and ratify their covenant.

On both sides of the Beer-sheba valley, in the Negeb, there is evidence of human settlement going back to the Chalcolithic Age (later fourth millennium B.C.). The settlers at that time lived in subterranean pit-dwellings and not only manufactured

The flat plains of the Negeb near Beersheba in southern Israel.

Excavations in progress at Tell es-Seba, biblical Beersheba. Archaeologists have found a planned and fortified city of the Judean monarchy.

articles of bone, flint and pottery but also, to some extent, copper. This period of settlement came to an end about 3000 B.C., a millennium before the time of Abraham.

The ancient Beer-sheba lay about four miles east of the modern city of the same name. There Abraham planted a tamarisk tree and called on the name of the Lord, the Everlasting God – the last phrase being the English rendering of El-'Olam (Gen. 21.33). It is probably implied that he also

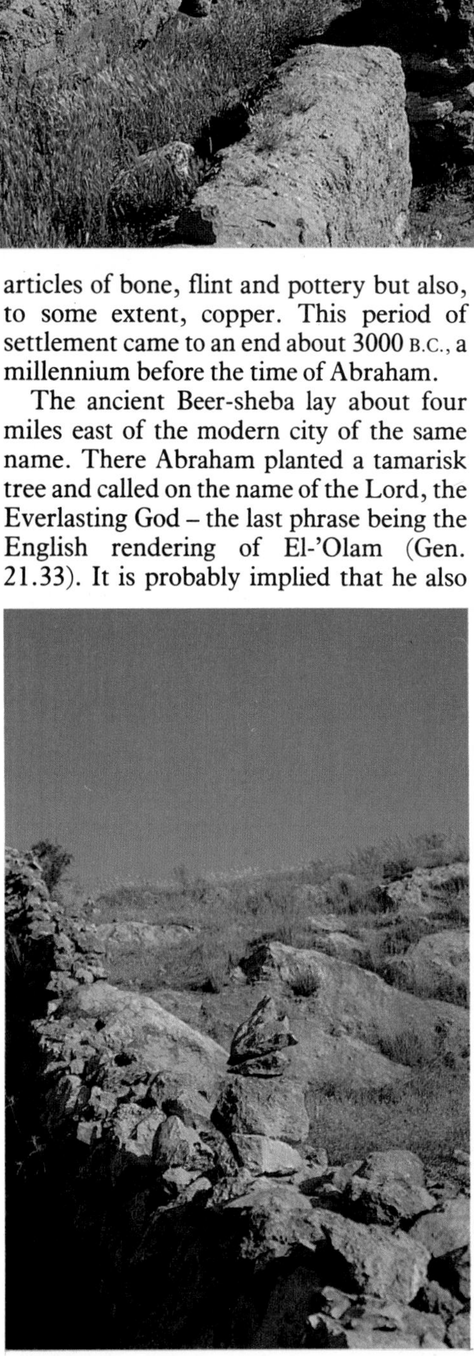

These boundary stones marking the limits of land-ownership are near Beersheba.

built an altar there, as Isaac did later (Gen. 26.25). He lived there for lengthy periods from time to time, as also did Isaac (Gen. 26.23-33). It was from Beer-sheba that Jacob set out for his long exile in Haran (Gen. 28.10); it was at Beer-sheba, many years later, that he halted briefly on his journey down to Egypt 'and offered sacrifices to the God of his father Isaac' (Gen. 46.1). The name of Isaac was apparently associated with Beer-sheba even more closely than the name of Abraham; apart from Isaac's residence there in manhood, it was from Beer-sheba that he had set out as a youth with his father Abraham to go to the place of sacrifice in 'the land of Moriah' (Gen. 22.1-19).

After the Israelite occupation of Canaan, Beer-sheba came to be regarded as the southern limit of the Israelites' settlement, or perhaps as the southern limit of the Canaanite land which they occupied, as in the expression 'from Dan to Beer-sheba' (Judg. 20.1, etc.) or 'from Beer-sheba to Dan' (1 Chron. 21.2, etc.). In Josh. 15.28 it is reckoned to the tribal territory of Judah; in Josh. 19.2 it is reckoned to the tribe of Simeon (which was early absorbed by Judah). The fact that Samuel's sons served as judges in Beer-sheba (1 Sam. 8.2) may indicate that Beer-sheba was recognized as a sanctuary, like the place to which Samuel himself went on circuit for the administration of justice (1 Sam. 7.16,17). Under the divided monarchy Beer-sheba belonged to the kingdom of Judah: it was Elijah's first stopping place when he fled from Jezebel's threats on his way south to Mount Horeb (1 Kings 19.3). After the return from the Babylonian exile, Beer-sheba was reoccupied by Jews (Neh. 11.27).

In Israel today the modern city of Beer-sheba is the capital of the Negeb.

Excavations began on the site of the ancient city (Tell Beer-sheba) in 1969 and laid bare a well planned city of the time of David and Solomon, which was evidently the centre of administration for that part of the kingdom in which it lay. It was a strongly defended city, but it could not hold out against the Assyrian siege-engines: Beer-sheba was one of the 'fortified cities of Judah' which Sennacherib reduced in 701 B.C. (2 Kings 18.13; Isa. 36.1). Shortly before this destruction of the city, there had been a temple there – the shrine or 'high place' whose existence is implied in Amos 5.5; 8.14. This temple had been dismantled as part of Hezekiah's reformation of religion (2 Kings 18.4); the altar of burnt-offering, however, complete with its 'horns', was discovered in 1973 while the storehouse walls were being excavated. In front of the city gate there was a well of unusual depth, excavated to a depth of 65 feet. This could conceivably have been the well dug by Abraham (Gen. 21.30), stopped up by the local inhabitants (Gen. 26.18) and re-opened by Isaac (Gen. 26.25-33).

A 'four horned' altar from the Canaanite period discovered at Beersheba.

It does not appear, however, that there

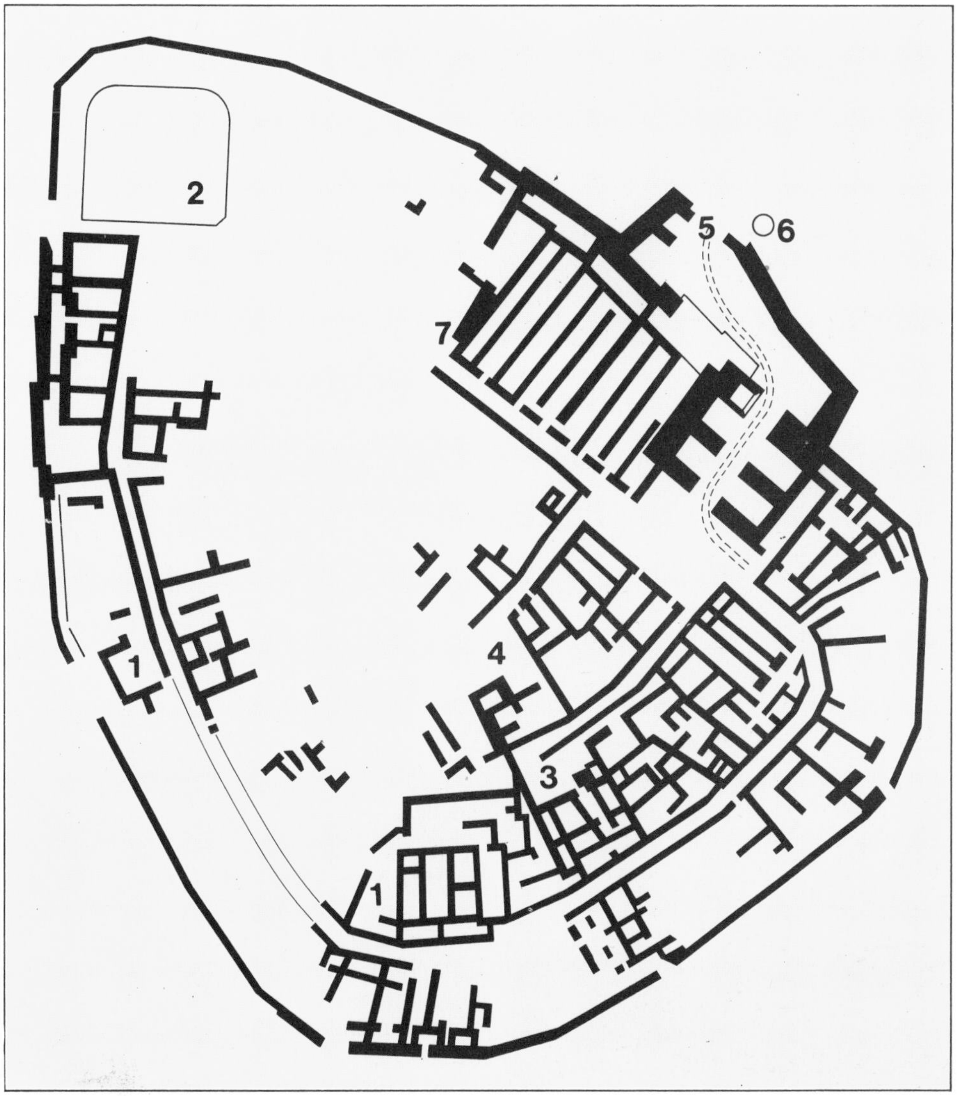

The excavated area of the city of Beersheba.

1 **Dwellings**
2 **Water system**
3 **Public buildings**
4 **Governor's palace**
5 **Outer gate**
6 **Well**
7 **Storehouses**

A painted pot from the Chalcolithic Period, preserved in the Negeb Museum, Beersheba.

A view of the Judean Hills in the vicinity of Beersheba.

was a city at Beer-sheba in Abraham's time, nor indeed throughout the Canaanite period. The Beer-sheba valley and its neighbourhood were frequented by pastoralists like Abraham because the water-table was sufficiently high to be tapped by the digging of wells.

Biblical references Gen. 21.25-33; 26.25 – The presence of God was not manifested at Beer-sheba by any sacred objects when Abraham, and later Isaac, worshipped there. There was a tree, but Abraham planted it; there was a well, but Abraham dug it; there was an altar, but Isaac built it. Abraham met God there without any visible token of the divine presence. Nor was Abraham the first to meet God there, according to the present sequence of the narrative. Hagar, the expelled slave-girl, met him there at a time of desperate need and distress, when her son Ishmael was on the point of dying of thirst 'in the wilderness of Beer-sheba'. God heard the crying boy, and showed Hagar a well of water (Gen. 21.14-21).

Machpelah

The cave Machpelah means 'the double cave'; so it is rendered in the Greek and Latin versions of Genesis, and rightly so, because the cave does contain two chambers. The name appears to have been extended from the cave (to which it primarily belongs) to the field in which it lay, and then to the surrounding area. The site is located 'near Mamre' (Gen. 23.17,19; 49.30). In the cave the patriarchs Abraham, Isaac and Jacob were buried, together with their wives.

A detailed account of Abraham's acquisition of the field is given in Gen. 23.3-20. When Sarah his wife died, Abraham owned not even a square foot of land in Canaan (although the whole country had been promised to him and his descendants) and so he found it necessary to buy a burial-place. He was then living at Mamre. He bought a suitable piece of ground from its owner, Ephron the Hittite, through the

Bedouin tribesmen at market. Hebron today is an important centre for Arabs in southern Israel.

good offices of other Hittites who were friends and neighbours of his own. The identity of these people's ethnic designation with that of the Indo-European Hittites who about this time were beginning to lay the foundation of their power in Asia Minor may be no more than a coincidence. It has been argued, indeed, that the details of the conveyance of the property to Abraham conform to the Hittite law-code of Asia Minor, but in fact they represent the common practice throughout the ancient Near East. The transaction was formally concluded at the gate of Ephron's city, in the presence of the elders of the populace and passers-by in general. If, as seems likely, the city of Hebron did not yet exist as such, the 'city' would be one of the four places which in due course came together to form the federation of Hebron.

As the transaction proceeds, sordid questions of payment are waved aside.

Abraham is welcome to accept as a gift not only the cave as a burial-place but the field which contained it. The field, to be sure, is worth 400 silver shekels, but what is that between friends? (It has been suggested that, by insisting on Abraham's acceptance of the field as well as the cave, Ephron wished to transfer certain public responsibilities from himself to Abraham, but we cannot be sure of this.) The contract is carefully recorded and witnessed: not only the cave and the field but 'all the trees that were in the field' were made over to Abraham. This was not a superfluous detail: to this day a Palestinian landowner may bequeath a field to one member of his family, the trees to another, and the right to gather the fruit of the trees to yet another – though this last refinement does not figure in Abraham's transaction with Ephron. For all the talk about Abraham's receiving the property as a gift, he knows what is

Modern Hebron. In the foreground can be seen the great *Haram el-Halil* – 'The Enclosure of the Friend', the Muslim shrine where it is said the patriarchs were buried.

expected of him, so he weighs out the 400 shekels of silver – not coins but ingots of silver, weighing in all 10 pounds avoirdupois or 4½ kilograms.

When Abraham himself died, some years later, he was buried in the same cave by his sons Ishmael and Isaac (Gen. 25.9,10). Isaac was later buried there by *his* two sons, Esau and Jacob (Gen. 35.27-29); and Jacob on his deathbed in Egypt charged Joseph to bury him there: 'There they buried Abraham and Sarah his wife; there they buried Isaac and Rebekah his wife; and there I buried Leah' (Gen 49.31).

It is remarkable, by the way, that Leah, the less well loved of Jacob's two wives, nevertheless shared his burial-place; the beloved Rachel had died years before, in giving birth to Benjamin, and 'was buried on the way to Ephrath (that is, Bethlehem)' (Gen. 35.19); her tomb is still shown on the right hand side of the main road from Jerusalem to Bethlehem. Jacob's body, then, was carried to Canaan by his sons and buried 'in the cave of the field at Machpelah, near Mamre' (Gen. 50.13).

No further mention is made of the place in the Old Testament, but it was not forgotten. The Book of Jubilees, a re-telling of events from the creation to the Exodus, produced in the first or second century B.C., says that Jacob buried Leah 'to the left of Sarah's grave', and this statement could depend on local knowledge. Josephus, writing in the seventies of the first century A.D., says that the patriarchs' tombs are shown in Hebron 'to this day, of really fine marble and of exquisite workmanship'.

The area, known for centuries as the Harem el-Halil (Arabic for 'the sacred enclosure of the Friend', i.e., Abraham), has been surrounded for the last 2,000 years by a magnificent stone wall, about 39 feet high and 8 feet thick, whose stones (some of which are 23 feet long) are characteristic of Herodian masonry. Although no positive statement has come down to us ascribing the building of the wall to Herod, his interest in his ancestor Abraham (shown, for example, at Mamre) would make it natural for him to honour his memory in this way. The enclosure itself is nearly 200 feet long by 100 feet broad. It may have been Herod, too, who built the marble monuments described by Josephus.

The Bordeaux pilgrim, describing his visit to the Holy Land in A.D. 333, says that at Hebron 'there is a remarkably beautiful tomb, square and made of stone, in which are laid Abraham, Isaac and Jacob, and Sarah, Rebekah and Leah'.

The monument or monuments marking the burial-place seem to have remained exposed to the sky, within their enclosure, until the latter half of the sixth century. Then, perhaps by direction of the Emperor Justinian (527-565), a great church-builder, a basilica was built over the burial-place of Isaac and Rebekah, in the eastern part of the enclosure. After the Arab conquest of Palestine in the seventh century the basilica was converted to a mosque, but the Jews of Hebron were allowed to pray within the enclosure. During the Crusader domination of the land in the twelfth century the building was restored to Christian use. In 1119 the bones of the patriarchs are said to have been discovered in excavations beneath the church and the courtyard. When they were reinterred, their names, with those of their wives, are said to have been inscribed on the sarcophagi in which the bones were placed.

With the expulsion of the Crusaders, the

Part of the masonry of the *Haram el-Halil* dates from Herodian times. It is built over the Cave of Machpelah.
Inset: The interior of Abraham's Mosque *(Haram el-Halil)* Hebron.

There is a viewing hole in the floor of Abraham's Mosque. Pious Jews push slips of paper with prayers written on them into the Cave of Machpelah itself, where the patriarchs are reputed to have been buried.

building became a mosque again, and so it remains to this day. In 1267 the Sultan Baybars prohibited Jews and Christians from praying within the enclosure; Jews were permitted to insert written prayers into the cave from the outside through a hole in the east wall.

The modern city of Hebron, called El-Halil ('the Friend') by Arabs has grown up since Crusader times around the enclosure. The ancient Hebron was situated farther west, on the hill Er-Rumeideh.

Since Israel gained control of Hebron as a result of the six-days war in 1967, Jews have once again obtained right of access to the enclosure and are permitted to hold regular services there.

Through a twelve-inch hole in the floor of the mosque visitors may look down into one of the two chambers of the double cave – the eastern chamber, in which the sarcophagi of Isaac and Rebekah stand. Through this hole, in accordance with Muslim custom, an oil lamp, perpetually lit, is lowered. A British officer, Col. Richard Meinertzhagen, was able to get down into the chamber when Hebron was taken from the Turks in 1917, and recorded what he saw – not very much, because of the darkness (relieved only by the light of his pipe, which he smoked sitting on one of the sarcophagi).

Otherwise the patriarchs and matriarchs appear to have been left undisturbed since Crusader times – Isaac and Rebekah directly under the mosque, and Abraham and Sarah, Jacob and Leah in the adjoining chamber under the forecourt. Despite the lack of reference to the site from patriarchal times, its authenticity may be regarded as certain.

Biblical references Exod. 3.6 – By the time God introduced himself to Moses at the burning bush as 'the God of Abraham, the God of Isaac and the God of Jacob', these patriarchs had been dead and buried for centuries. But Jesus deduced the truth of resurrection from these words of God: 'he is not God of the dead, but of the living; for all live to him' (Luke 20.38).

Bedouin tribesmen in the Negeb.

A nomad family on the move.

Places David knew

The Israelite Kingdom

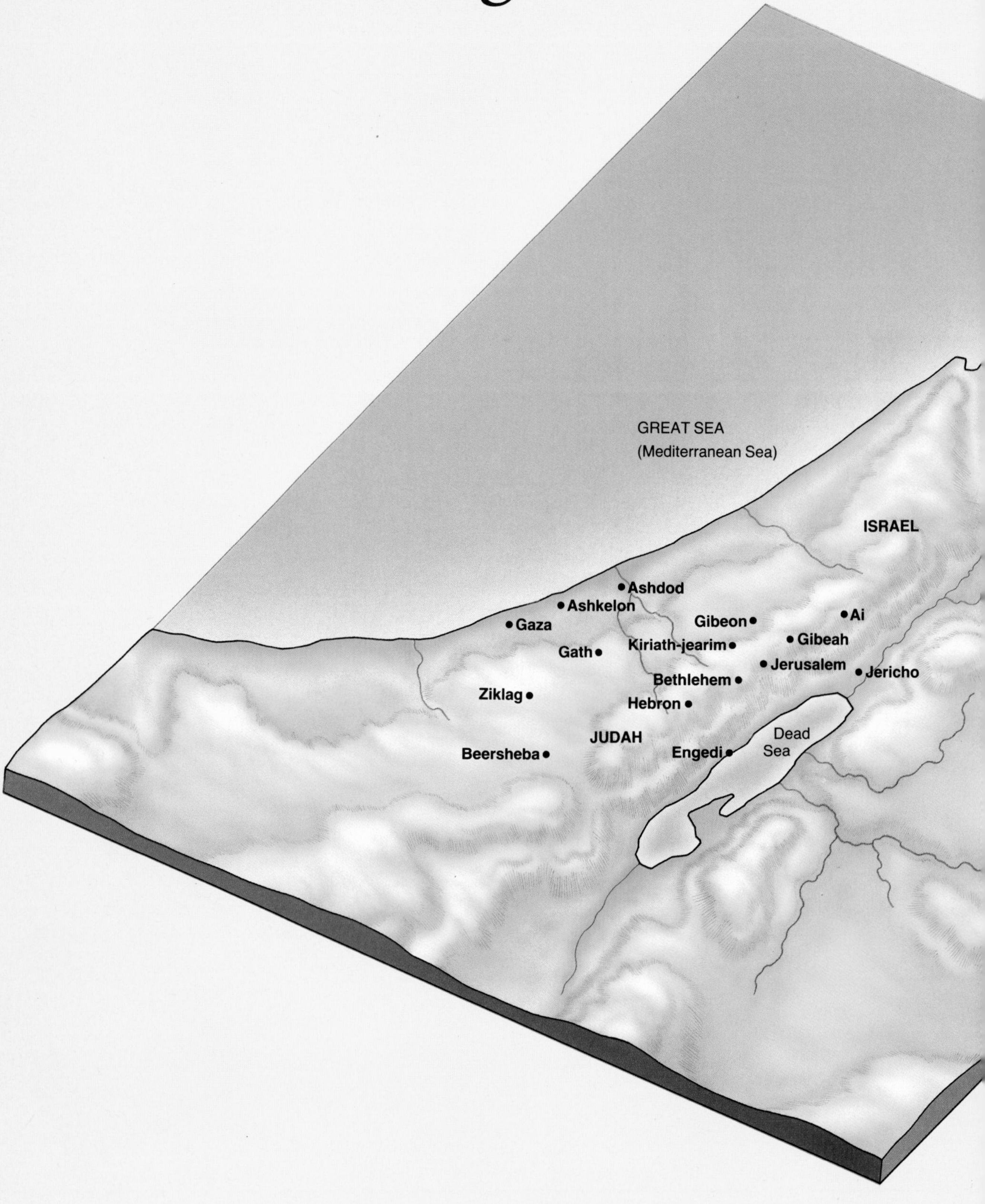

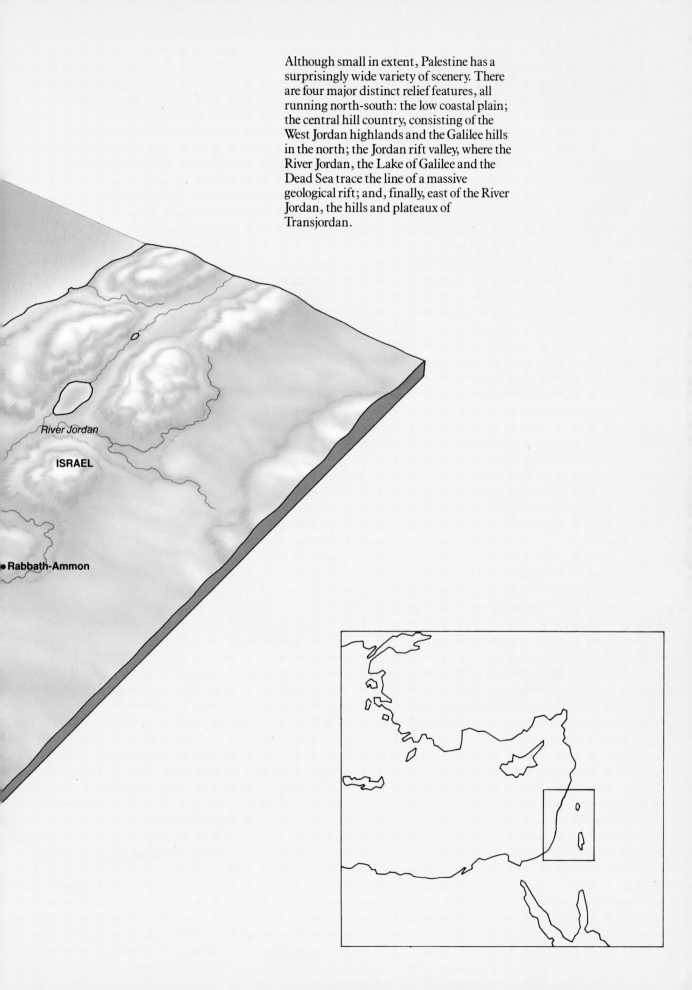

Although small in extent, Palestine has a surprisingly wide variety of scenery. There are four major distinct relief features, all running north-south: the low coastal plain; the central hill country, consisting of the West Jordan highlands and the Galilee hills in the north; the Jordan rift valley, where the River Jordan, the Lake of Galilee and the Dead Sea trace the line of a massive geological rift; and, finally, east of the River Jordan, the hills and plateaux of Transjordan.

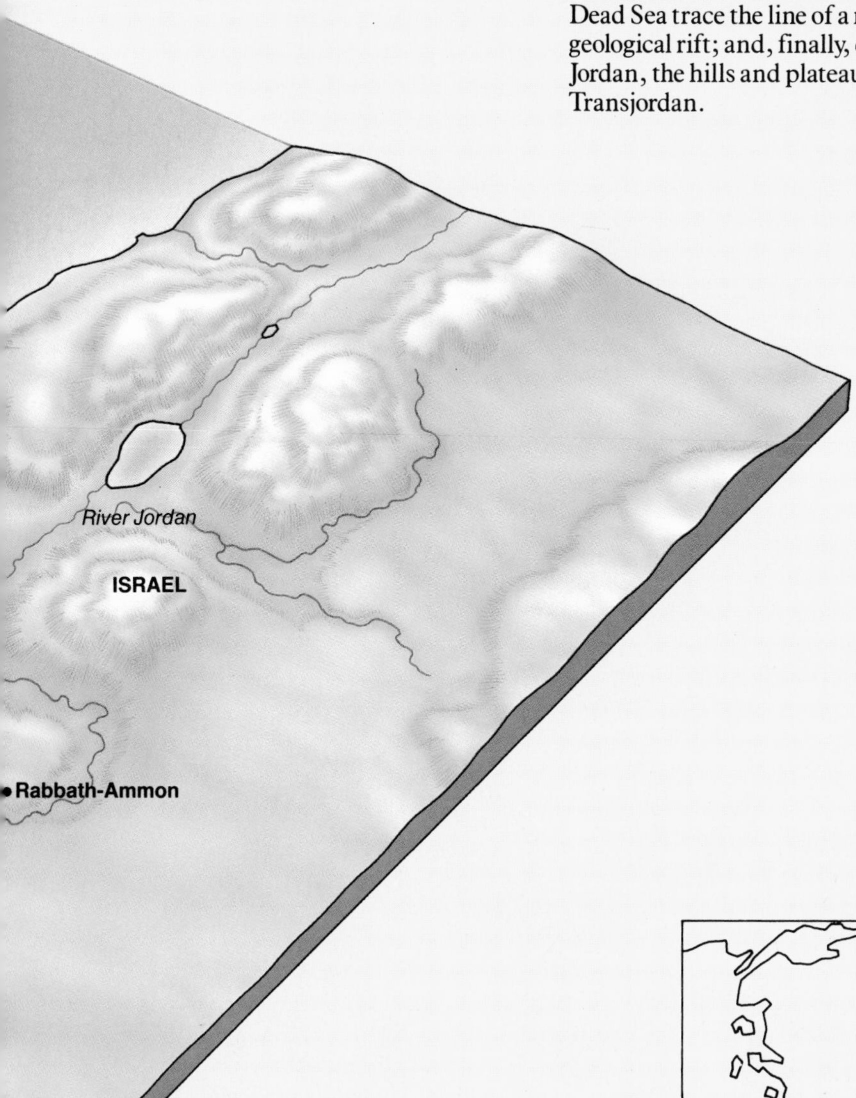

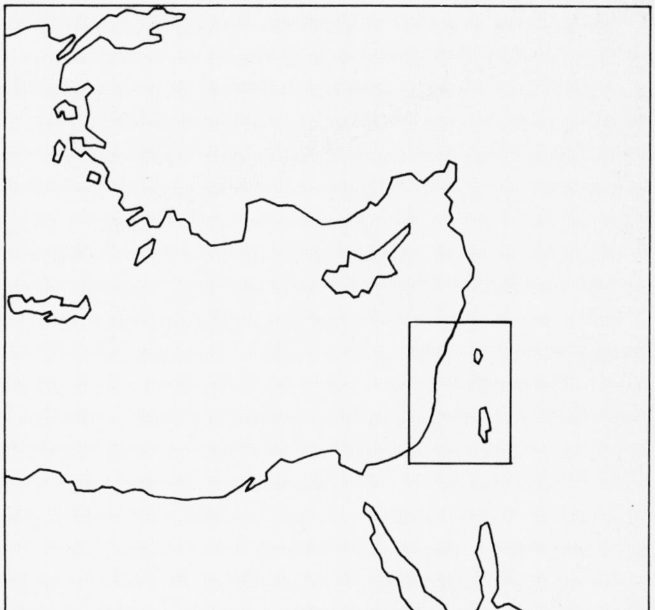

Introduction

David lived nearly 1,000 years after the time of Abraham. The land in which he lived was the land in which Abraham and spent most of his life. But many changes had taken place in the meantime. Abraham had moved as a nomad through the land of Canaan; the only part of it that he owned was the field near Hebron which he bought from its owners to bury Sarah there. Some centuries later, however, Abraham's descendants, the Israelites, settled in the land and occupied more and more of it. It was David who, about 1000 BC, completed that work of occupation and established his rule over it 'from Dan to Beersheba'.

Between Abraham's time and David's a succession of imperial powers rose and fell in the Near East. The absence of any great superpower on his frontiers – a rare circumstance indeed – enabled David to extend his authority beyond the land of Israel and create a short-lived empire stretching from the Egyptian border to the Euphrates.

We begin, then, with Bethlehem, David's birthplace, and go on to look at other places associated with his career. By far the most outstanding of these is Jerusalem. It was David who, by capturing Jerusalem early in his reign and making it his capital, did as much as anyone in history has done to give that city the importance which it retains to our own day.

F. F. BRUCE

Bethlehem

Bethlehem is important in Old Testament story as the birthplace of King David, just as in the New Testament it is important as the birthplace of Jesus, 'great David's greater Son'.

It is sometimes called more precisely 'Bethlehem in Judah' (e.g. Judg. 17.7; 19.1; Ruth 1.1), because there was (and still is) another Bethlehem, in Galilee (Josh. 19.15). It was the most northerly settlement of the tribe of Judah – Jerusalem, which lies five and a half miles to the north of it, was nominally allotted to the tribe of Benjamin (Josh. 18.27), though it did not come under Israelite control until the time of David.

There is evidence of some human presence on the site of Bethlehem in prehistoric times, but there could be no effective settlement there until the technique of digging cisterns for the collection of water had been devised, for there is no natural spring in Bethlehem. Continuous

A bedouin shepherd today.

settlement began in the Late Bronze Age (some time after 1600 B.C.). East of the Church of the Nativity there is a mound with surface pottery from the Late Bronze and Iron Ages; this may mark the site of the Canaanite city. The name Bethlehem is Canaanite in origin; it appears to have meant 'house of Lahmu' (a Canaanite divinity) but it was later understood to mean 'house of Bread' (*lehem* being the Hebrew word for bread).

An alternative name for the place in early days was Ephrath: the members of its best-known family in Old Testament history are called 'Ephrathites from Bethlehem in Judah' (Ruth 1.2). It is first mentioned in the biblical record as the place near which Rachel died, after giving birth to Benjamin – 'and she was buried on the way to Ephrath (that is, Bethlehem), and Jacob set up a pillar upon her grave; it is the pillar of Rachel's tomb, which is there to this day' (Gen. 35.19,20). The traditional place of

her burial is still to be seen to the right-hand side of the road from Jerusalem to Bethlehem, about a mile north of Bethlehem; the pillar set up by Jacob has long since disappeared, but has been replaced by a domed structure.

Bethlehem figures in two stories which form appendices to the book of Judges. It was a young Levite from Bethlehem whom Micah installed as priest in his 'house of gods' in the hill country of Ephraim (Judg.

A shepherd tends his flock on a barren hillside near Bethlehem.

Even today bedouin peasants harvest the corn by hand. Both men and women gather in the grain.

Interior of the Church of the Nativity, Bethlehem.

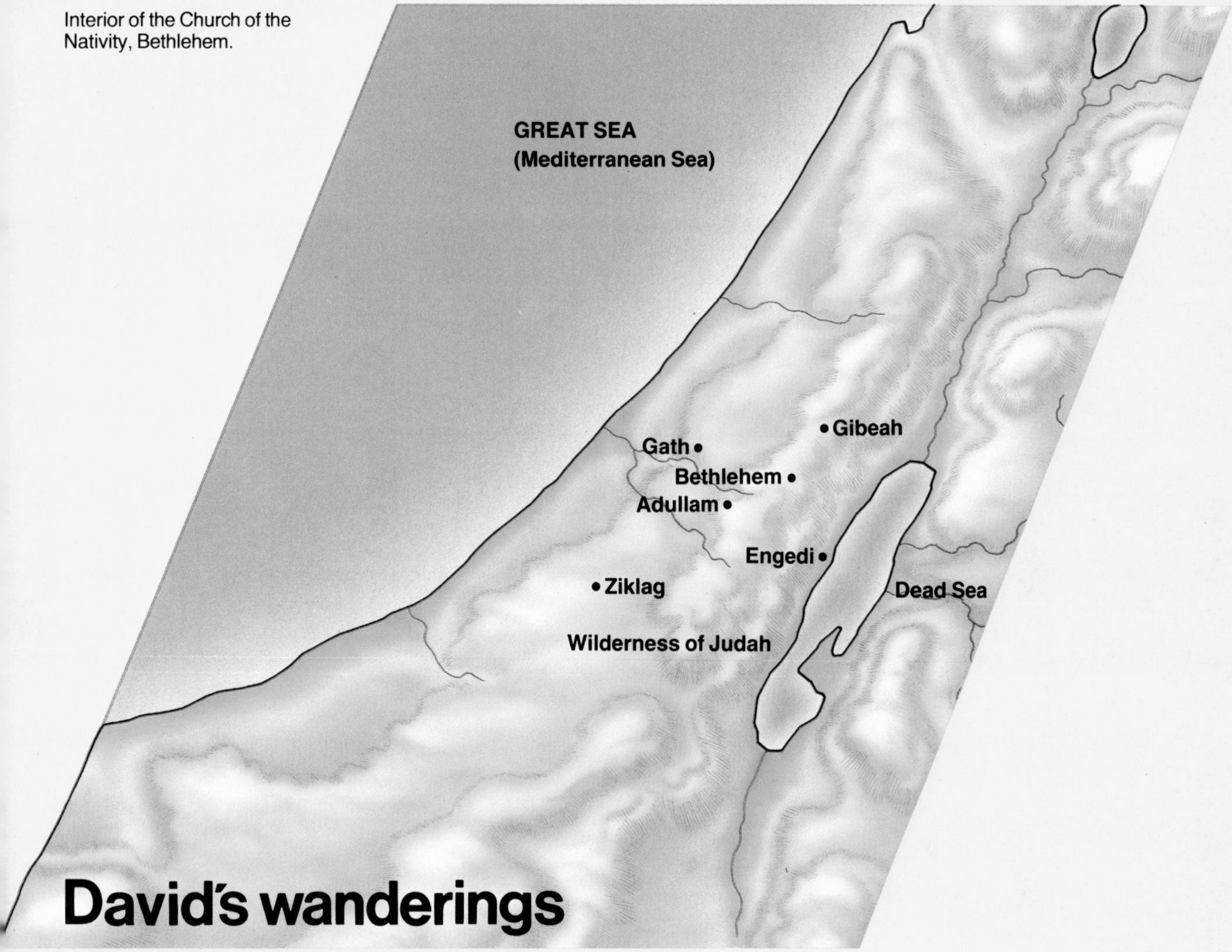

17.7-13), but he was persuaded by the Danites to accompany them on their northward migration to find a new home near the sources of Jordan; there he became chief priest to the tribe of Dan. Although his home was Bethlehem, he did not belong to the tribe of Judah; he was a descendant of Moses (Judg. 18.30). Again, it was from Bethlehem, the home of his father-in-law, that another Levite set out with his concubine to return to his residence in the hill country of Ephraim – a disastrous journey, as it turned out (Judg. 19.1-21).

To the period of the judges belongs also the happier story told in the book of Ruth, for which Bethlehem provides the setting. It was from Bethlehem that Elimelech and his family set out for Moab in Transjordan in a time of famine; it was to Bethlehem that his widow Naomi returned ten years later with her devoted daughter-in-law Ruth. Naomi's wise counsel made it possible for Ruth to become the wife of Boaz, a prosperous landowner of Bethlehem and a kinsman of her late husband. The firstborn

Olive groves near Bethlehem.

Pious Jews sit in front of the reputed Tomb of Rachel, two miles from Bethlehem.

child of this marriage was Obed, whose son Jesse was David's father. The fact that David's great-grandmother came originally from Moab has been thought to explain David's entrusting his parents to the care of the king of Moab when he was fleeing from King Saul (1 Sam. 22.3,4).

Not only was David himself born in Bethlehem; it was the birthplace of a number of his relatives, including the three sons of his sister Zeruiah – Joab, Abishai and Asahel. When Asahel was killed by Abner in the fighting that followed Saul's death, it was in his family tomb in Bethlehem that he was buried (2 Sam. 2.32).

Jesse, David's father, was a landowner and sheep-rearer of Bethlehem. David (born about 1040 B.C.) was his youngest son; he was secretly anointed king over Israel in his father's house by the prophet Samuel while King Saul was still alive. If Saul had no positive knowledge of Samuel's action,

he probably suspected something of the kind and this would have contributed to his hostility against David. But David was at one time a favourite of Saul's: he was appointed court musician and later, after his victory over the Philistine Goliath, he became captain of the royal bodyguard for a few months and was given Michal, Saul's daughter, as his wife.

After his attachment to Saul's court and his subsequent life as a refugee and guerrilla leader in the wilderness of Judah, David's contacts with Bethlehem were infrequent (*cf.* 1 Sam. 20.6,28,29). One incident that receives honourable mention is the courageous exploit of his three 'mighty men' who broke through the Philistines' lines at the risk of their lives to fetch David some water from the well by the city gate of Bethlehem when he expressed a longing for it. 'The garrison of the Philistines was then at Bethlehem.' When the men brought the

This little domed building was built in the eighteenth century to cover the supposed site of Rachel's tomb. Like most of the 'holy places' of modern Israel, it is constantly guarded against terrorist activities.

Part of the modern town of Bethlehem.

Bethlehem from the campanile of the Church of the Nativity.

water back to David in the cave of Adullam he poured it out as a libation: water so dearly procured was too sacred for him to drink in gratification of a personal craving (2 Sam. 23.13-17).

Bethlehem was one of the cities in Judah fortified by Rehoboam, Solomon's son and successor, when he found himself left with a kingdom comprising only the tribal territories of Judah and Benjamin (2 Chron. 11.6). But it was in itself an unimportant place and plays no part in the history of the kings of Judah. Yet, when the fortunes of the dynasty of David had fallen on evil days, the prophet Micah looked to Bethlehem as the place from which a ruler would come to restore the former glories:

But you, O Bethlehem Ephrathah,
who are little to be among the clans of Judah,
from you shall come forth for me
one who is to be ruler in Israel,
whose origin is from of old,
from ancient days. (Mic. 5.2)

The Gospels tell us how this hope was fulfilled (*cf.* Matt. 2.5,6).

Biblical references Genesis 35.16-20 – Rachel's death and burial on the way to Bethlehem.
Ruth 1-4 – Most of the story of Ruth is set in Bethlehem. The whole book is worth reading: it is not long.
1 Samuel 16.1-13 – David anointed king by Samuel in his father's home at Bethlehem.
2 Samuel 23.13-17 – David's followers fetch him water from the well at Bethlehem at the risk of their lives.
Micah 5.2 – Bethlehem: the birthplace of the coming King.

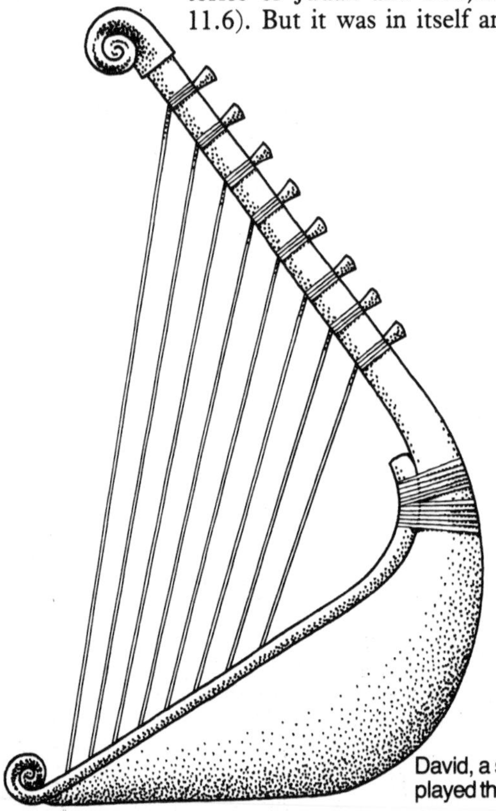

David, a skilled musician, played the harp or lyre (kinnor).

Gibeah

Gibeah, standing on the main road from Judah and Jerusalem north into the central highlands of Ephraim, was the chief town in the tribal territory of Benjamin – 'Gibeah, which belongs to Benjamin' (Judg. 19.14). It is generally identified with Tell el-Ful, a mound standing on a hill 2,754 feet high, 3 miles north of Jerusalem. David knew it because Saul had his residence there: it is called 'Gibeah of Saul' in 1 Sam. 11.4 and Isa. 10.29. When David was summoned to Saul's court to play soothing music to him on the lyre and later to become his armour-bearer, it was to Gibeah that he went (1 Sam. 16.14-23).

A few generations earlier, Gibeah had been the scene of a shocking breach of the covenant which bound the tribes of Israel together. A Levite and his Bethlehemite concubine were treated so abominably when they sought overnight hospitality there that the other tribes demanded that the tribe of Benjamin should give up the perpetrators of the outrage for judgment and execution. Only so would it be possible to 'put away evil from Israel' (Judg. 20.13). The leaders of Benjamin refused this demand, so the other tribes declared a holy war against Benjamin. Gibeah was destroyed, and the tribe of Benjamin itself was nearly wiped out. 'The day of Gibeah' was remembered for centuries as a day of shame and disaster (Hos. 9.9; 10.9).

When calmer counsels prevailed, measures were taken to save the tribe of Benjamin from annihilation: among other things, wives were found for some of its survivors from Jabesh-gilead, east of the Jordan (Judg. 21.14). A bond of kinship was thus forged between the people of Benjamin and Jabesh-gilead, and this may explain Saul's promptness in taking military action on behalf of the men of Jabesh-gilead at the beginning of his reign when they were threatened with mutilation and enslavement (1 Sam. 11.1-11). It may explain also their

Tell el-Ful, about three miles north of Jerusalem, is almost certainly the biblical Gibeah of Saul. A small fortress was erected there about the time of King Saul.

courageous rescue of Saul's dead body and those of his sons from the wall of Beth-shan where they had been exposed by the Philistines, in order to give them decent burial (1 Sam. 30.11-13).

Gibeah was rebuilt after its destruction in the holy war, and it was there that Saul's family lived. When Saul became king, he continued to live in Gibeah. He no doubt extended and fortified his farmhouse, but there was nothing palatial about his royal residence. It was to Gibeah that he returned after Samuel anointed him king (1 Sam. 10.26), and it was there that messengers came to tell him of the desperate plight of the people of Jabesh-gilead (1 Sam. 11.4). Michmash, where the Philistines had a garrison at the time, lay across the valley to the north-north-east, between five and six miles as the crow flies; it was from Gibeah that Saul's watchmen saw the panic-stricken commotion of the garrison at Michmash on the occasion when Jonathan, Saul's son, attacked it (1 Sam. 14.16). It was to Gibeah, again, that Saul returned after Samuel had denounced him as no longer fit to reign over Israel (1 Sam. 15.34) and it was to Gibeah, after David had become a fugitive, that reports were brought to Saul from time to time about David's whereabouts (1 Sam. 22.6; 23.19; 26.1).

A peasant woman gathers the sheaves of corn at harvest time.

A good deal of the history of the site has been brought to light by excavations on Tell el-Ful. In 1868 Sir Charles Warren did some exploratory work there on behalf of the Palestine Exploration Fund, but the first thorough excavation was carried out under the direction of W. F. Albright in 1922-23 (and again in 1933 and 1964) on behalf of the American School of Oriental Research in Jerusalem. (The 1964 season was conducted jointly with P. W. Lapp on behalf of Pittsburgh Theological Seminary.) Five main periods of occupation were identified; the second, third and fourth of these were accompanied by stone fortifications. The first of the five was an Iron Age settlement which came to an end about 1100 B.C.; it is probably the Gibeah which was destroyed in the inter-tribal war described in Judg. 20.19-48. The second period (11th century B.C.) was marked by two successive stages of fortification – perhaps the stone fortress built by Saul was later repaired by David. (Another possibility is that a Philistine fortress, one of a series built to control the main roads through the country, was taken over and occupied by Saul.) From the second stage comes one of the earliest known iron implements from Israelite times – an iron plough-tip. (We are told in 1 Sam. 13.19-22 that the Philistines retained the monopoly of iron-working in their own hands; Israelite farmers had to go to Philistine smiths to have their agricultural implements

Ploughing methods have changed very little since biblical times in some areas of Israel.

sharpened, and the only Israelites to have an iron sword-blade or spear-head were Saul and Jonathan.)

The third period of occupation at Gibeah belongs to the closing years of the Judean monarchy, from the late 8th to the early 6th century B.C. A new, smaller fortress built towards the end of the 8th century was certainly part of the work of Hezekiah in establishing strongpoints against the Assyrians; it was taken by Sennacherib's army (*cf.* Isa. 36.1). In Isa. 10.27-32 an Assyrian advance on Jerusalem from the north – not, it seems, Sennacherib's – is described, in the course of which 'Gibeah of Saul has fled'.

Gibeah was reoccupied and refortified in the following century, perhaps under Josiah; to this phase belong a number of earthenware jar-handles carrying the royal stamp. But this phase of settlement and fortification was abruptly terminated by the Babylonian invasion under Nebuchadnezzar (587 B.C.).

There was a further period of fortified occupation under Persian and Greek rule. Some pottery from the later part of this period (3rd and 2nd century B.C.) has come to light, together with three bronze coins of Ptolemy Philadelphus, king of Egypt (285-246 B.C.).

The fifth settlement on the site, in the early Roman period, was unwalled. It came to an end during the Jewish revolt against Rome which broke out in A.D. 66; Josephus reports that the Roman commander Titus spent the night at Gibeah before moving on to besiege Jerusalem in April, A.D. 70.

Today another royal residence stands on the slopes of the hill. King Hussein of Jordan had it built for himself in the 1960's, but the Six Days War of 1967 put an end to the construction and it remains unfinished.

Biblical references Judges 19.14-30 – Gibeah: the scene of outrage.
Judges 20.19-40 – Gibeah attacked and destroyed by the other tribes of Israel.
1 Samuel 10.10,26; 15.34; 22.6 – Gibeah: Saul's ancestral home and his headquarters as king of Israel.

Plan of the fortress excavated by archaeologists at Tell el-Ful (Gibeah), c 600 BC.

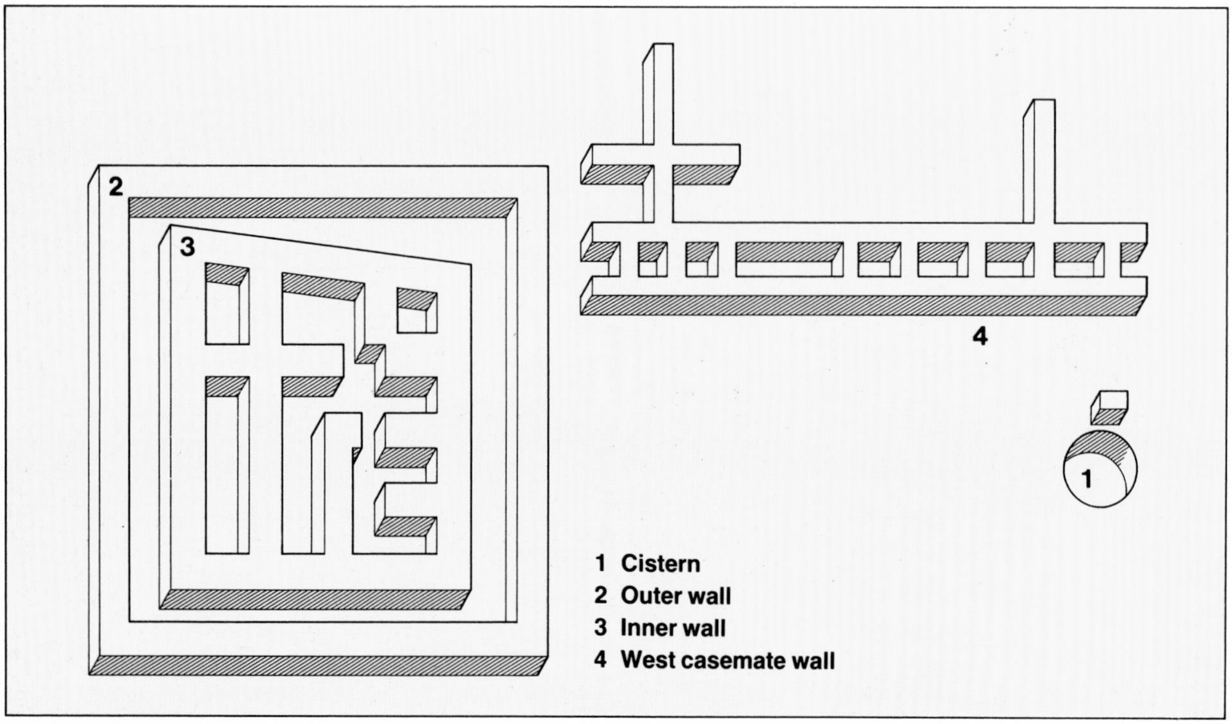

Wilderness of Judah

Barren hillside at Engedi, the country where David hid from King Saul.

The Cave of Adullam. During his period of outlawry, in the later part of Saul's reign, David was compelled to seek refuge in various places in the wilderness of Judah, moving from one to another as Saul tried to flush him out. Two places in this part of the country are specially associated with him: the cave of Adullam (1 Sam. 22.1) and the 'strongholds of Engedi' (1 Sam. 23.29).

Adullam was a Canaanite town in patriarchal times: Jacob's son Judah had a close friend called Hiram the Adullamite (Gen. 38.1). The king of Adullam was one of the Canaanite leaders overthrown by Joshua

The 'Goats' Spring', which was known in Old Testament times and which gives Engedi its name, supports rich vegetation.

(Josh. 12.15); Adullam was then allotted to the tribe of Judah (Josh. 15.35). It retained the same name throughout the period of the monarch (*cf.* its fortification by Rehoboam after the disruption of the kingdom, 2 Chron. 11.7). It was resettled after the return from the Babylonian exile (Neh. 11.30) and remained a Jewish town in the time of Judas Maccabaeus (2 Macc. 12.38). In the 4th century A.D. Eusebius, bishop of Caesarea, knew it as a large village ten miles east of Eleutheropolis (modern Beth-guvrin).

There are many caves in the region; some of them have a succession of inner recesses, capable of accommodating a considerable body of men, like the 400 who joined David there during his exile – not only his kinsmen but 'every one who was in distress, and every one who was in debt, and every one who was discontented' (1 Sam. 22.2). It was to the cave of Adullam that David's three friends brought him back water from the

well in Bethlehem (about thirteen miles to the north-east), risking their lives by going through the Philistine lines to fetch it (2 Sam. 23.13-17).

Engedi, 'the fountain of the kid', is a perennial spring on the west shore of the Dead Sea, rising about 650 feet above it and forming a large oasis (now one of the national parks of Israel). The desert area to the west of the oasis is called 'the wilderness of Engedi' (1 Sam. 24.1). There David established a fortified redoubt for himself and his companions for some time during his flight from Saul. It was in a cave in this neighbourhood that he once had a rare opportunity to make an end of Saul, but contented himself with cutting off a piece of his cloak, as evidence to Saul that he had spared his life when he had him at his mercy.

As for the oasis of Engedi, its fertility and beauty are reflected in Song of Songs 1.14, where the bride compares her beloved to 'a

A rich crop of grapes.

Sunset over the Judean Wilderness.

Inset: The barren hills of the Judean Wilderness stretch for miles into the far distance.

cluster of henna blossoms in the vineyards of Engedi'. Later, the author of Ecclesiasticus speaks of himself as having grown tall 'like a palm tree in Engedi' (Sir. 24.14).

Such an attractive place was likely to be settled from an early date. On a hill terrace above the spring, less than 500 feet to the north, a stone enclosure of the Chalcolithic Age (*c.* 3500 B.C.) was brought to light in 1956-57. It is believed to have enclosed a sacred area, containing buildings dedicated to some form of worship.

The outstanding archaeological site on the oasis is Tell Goren, where excavations extending over five seasons have revealed ample evidence of successive strata of occupation from the Judean monarchy to the Byzantine period. To the Byzantine period also belong the remains of a nearby synagogue, destroyed by fire early in the reign of Justinian (527-565). It proved to have been built over the remains of an earlier synagogue of the late 2nd and 3rd century A.D.

A striking rock-form caused by natural forces of erosion in the Judean Wilderness on the west shores of the Dead Sea.

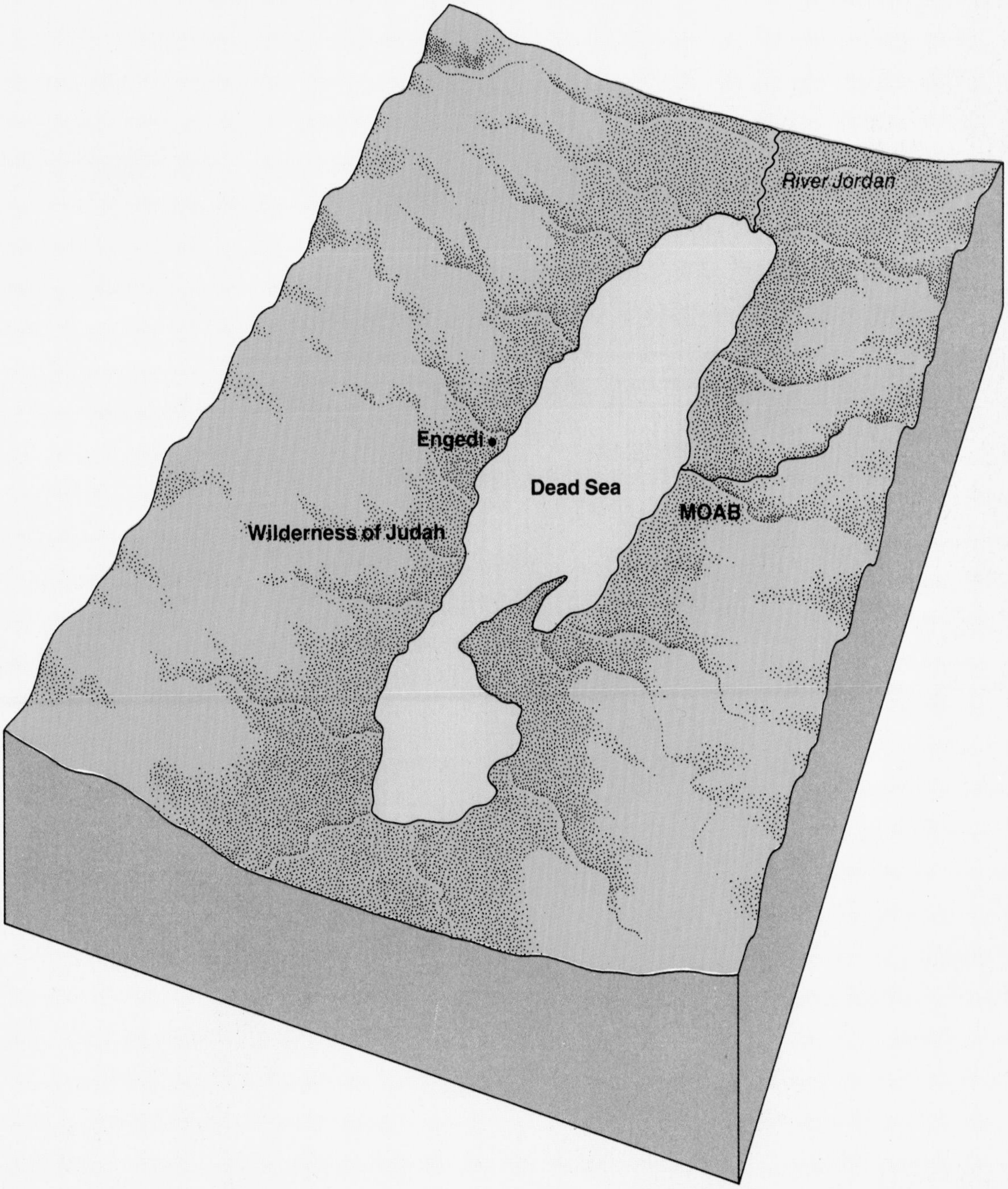

Other places in the wilderness of Judah which figure in David's adventures as a fugitive from Saul are Keilah (1 Sam. 23.1-13), three miles south of Adullam; the wilderness of Maon (1 Sam. 23.24,25), stretching some miles south of Ziph; the hill of Hachilah (1 Sam. 26.1), between Ziph and Engedi.

Biblical references 1 Samuel 22.1,2 – The cave of Adullam. Psalms 57 and 142 are said to have been composed by David when he was 'in the cave'.
1 Samuel 24 – An adventure in the wilderness of Engedi.
Psalm 63 – Said to have been composed by David 'when he was in the Wilderness of Judah'.

A dry stream-bed in the Judean Wilderness.

Cities of the Philistines

The Philistines invaded Canaan from the Mediterranean about the same time as the Israelites invaded it from the eastern desert. They belonged to the 'people of the sea' (as the Egyptians called them) who were forced by war or famine or some other natural disaster to leave their abodes in South West Asia Minor and Crete and to seek new homes. They were repulsed when they tried to land on Egyptian soil (*c.* 1200 B.C.) but they succeeded in establishing themselves at the southern end of the Mediterranean seaboard of Canaan. There they took over five cities which had previously been Canaanite. From south to north along the seaboard these were Gaza, Ashkelon and Ashdod, with Ekron farther inland, north-east from Ashdod, and Gath still farther inland, in an easterly direction from Ashkelon.

Each of these cities was ruled by one of 'the five lords of the Philistines' (Judg. 3.3, etc.). The word for 'lord' *seren*, probably belonged to the Philistine language; some think it is related to the Greek noun from which our work 'tyrant' is derived. But in the course of a few generations the Philistines spoke Canaanite and worshipped Canaanite divinities, like the grain-god Dagon. This may have been because the invading people of the sea were mostly men, who married Canaanite women. Language and religion are transmitted more by mothers than by fathers. But the Philistines

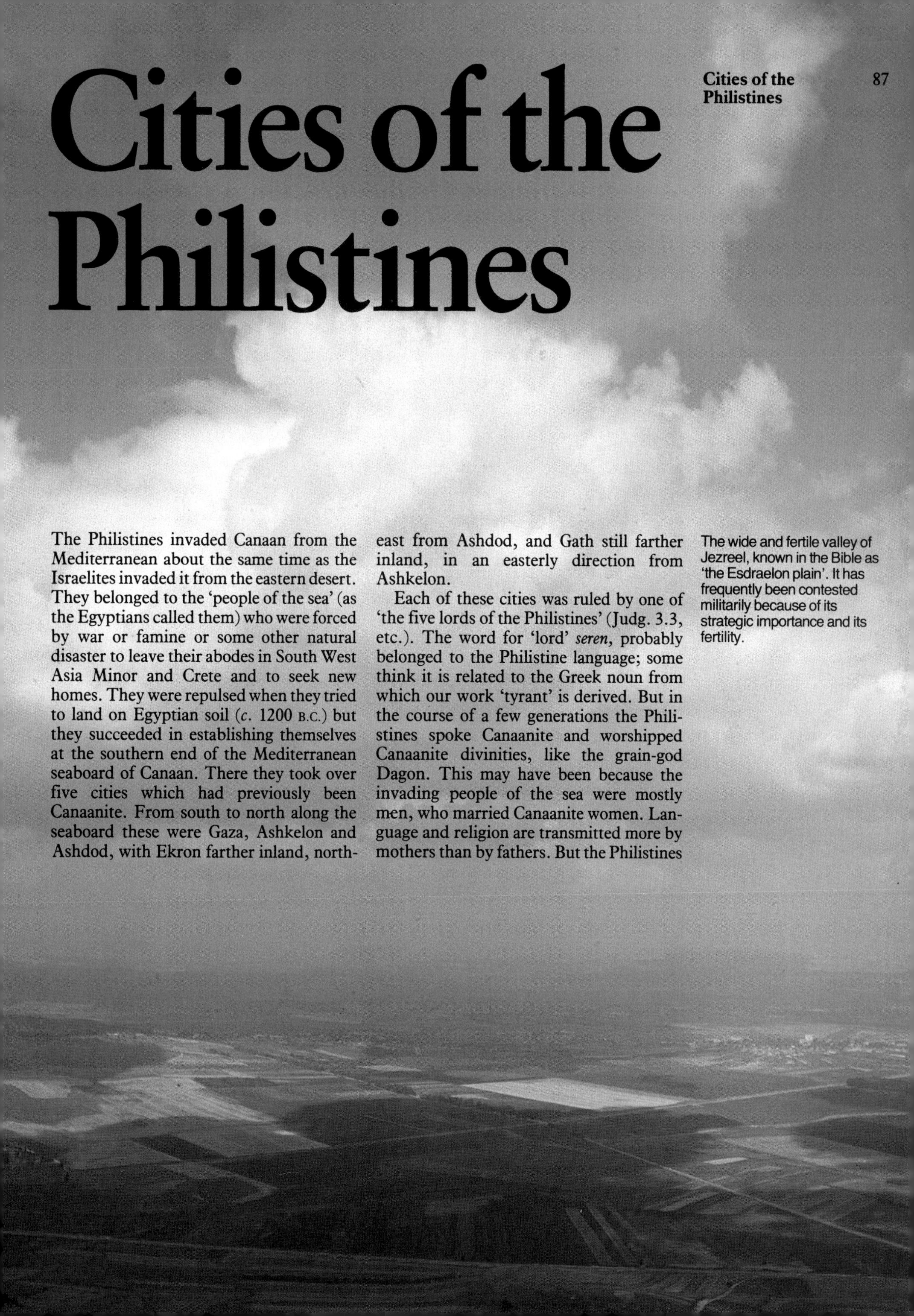

The wide and fertile valley of Jezreel, known in the Bible as 'the Esdraelon plain'. It has frequently been contested militarily because of its strategic importance and its fertility.

retained one cultural feature which distinguished them from the Canaanites, Hebrews and Egyptians: they did not practise circumcision. Hence the phrase 'uncircumcised Philistine' is a common one in the Old Testament – it is applied, for example, by David to Goliath in 1 Sam. 17.26.

The Philistines extended their control eastward and northward, ultimately penetrating the Plain of Jezreel as far as the Jordan valley and reducing many of the Israelites to subject status. It is plain from the story of Samson that life under the Philistines was not too hard for the Israelite peasantry, except when people like Samson stirred up trouble (Judg. 15.9-13).

It was largely to unify the tribes of Israel against their Philistine overlords that it was decided to have a king instead of judges. Saul, the first king of Israel, had some limited success against the Philistines. He met his death fighting them on Mount Gilboa in an endeavour to break through

An impressive portion of the wall of the fortress of Ashkelon, dating from the Crusades.

An artist's impression of the Ark of the Covenant.

the barrier which their garrisons in the Plain of Jezreel had erected between the central and the northern tribes.

After Saul's death the ascendancy of the Philistines seemed assured. They had no objection to David's appointment as king of Judah because they thought that he was their trusty vassal, unable to take any action without their permission. But it was thanks to David that their control of the country was broken, until at last the roles were reversed and they became vassals to him.

Of the Philistine cities, the one which David knew best was Gath, the site of which remains thus far unidentified. Its name is the Canaanite word for 'winepress' David's youthful exploit against Goliath of Gath did not bring him into contact with the giant's native place, but at a later stage he and his guerrilla band entered the service of Achish, king of Gath (1 Sam. 27.2). Achish greatly valued this augmentation of his military strength; before long he made David commander of his personal bodyguard. He allowed David and his men to settle in Ziklag, a city of the Negev, which remained the property of David's dynasty to the end of the monarchy (1 Sam. 27.6).

The other Philistine leaders, however, did not have so much confidence in David as Achish had, and on the eve of the battle of Mount Gilboa Achish had to yield to pressure from them and send David back to Ziklag. They argued with Achish that, if David entered the battle on their side, he would change sides during the fighting and go over to Saul, his former master, to the great detriment of the Philistines – which most probably is exactly what David would have done. At a later time David captured Gath in the course of his campaigns against the Philistines (1 Chron. 18.1; 20.6).

A Philistine warrior wearing a distinctive feather head-dress.

But David's association with the men of Gath (the Gittites) had long-enduring effects. It was among them that he recruited his own royal bodyguard, the Pelethites and Cherethites, together with a force of six hundred soliders, led by Ittai, whose loyalty to David was proved at the time of Absalom's rebellion (2 Sam. 15.18-22).

A stone sarcophagus of the Roman period at Ashkelon.

The Philistine city of Ashkelon lies beneath these coastal sand dunes. Modern Ashkelon is a popular seaside resort.

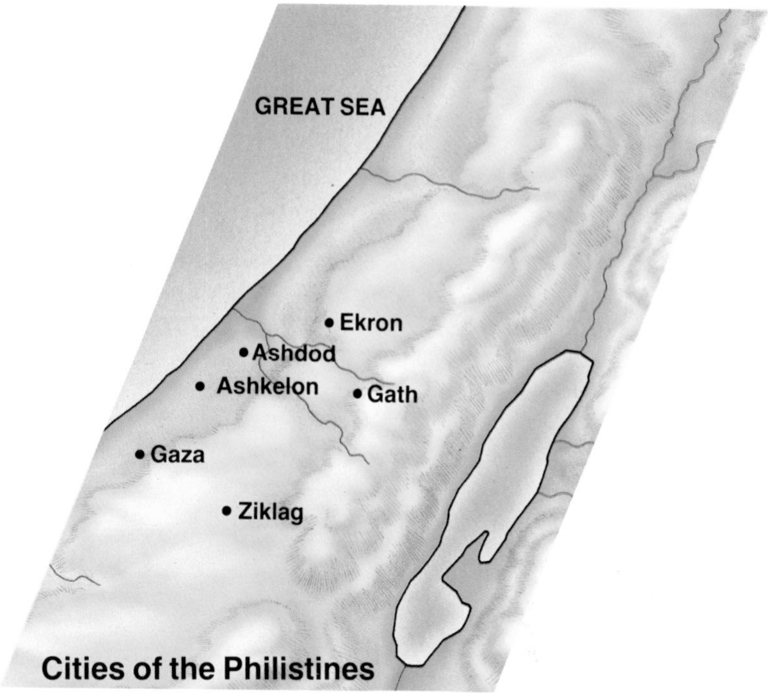

Another Gittite, Obed-edom by name, was given custody of the ark of the covenant for three months after the first abortive attempt to bring it from Kiriath-jearim to Jerusalem – 'and the Lord blessed Obed-edom and all his household' (2 Sam. 6.10-12).

Gath was fortified by Rehoboam (2 Chron. 11.8), but its walls were demolished by Uzziah (2 Chron. 26.6). The prophet Amos, towards the end of Uzziah's reign (*c.* 740 B.C.), knew it as a ruin (Amos 6.2). When David sang his dirge over Saul and Jonathan, on hearing of their death in the battle of Mount Gilboa, he said:

'Tell it not in Gath,
publish it not in the streets of Ashkelon.'
(2 Sam. 1.12)

Ashkelon was a Philistine city on the seacoast. Like other Philistine cities, it was Canaanite before it became Philistine. It is mentioned in Egyptian texts of the 19th century B.C. and it belonged to the Egyptian Empire for some centuries. It took part in a revolt against Egypt in the reign of Rameses II; his successor Merneptah (1234-1225 B.C.) claims to have reconquered it. (He records this claim in an inscription which is otherwise famous because it contains the first non-biblical mention of Israel.) Apart from the reference to it in David's dirge, Ashkelon is not mentioned in the records of his reign. It figures briefly in the story of Samson, two or three generations earlier (Judg. 14.19).

A Philistine city which figures more prominently in the story of Samson is Gaza.

An elaborate stone capital from the Roman period, excavated at Ashkelon.

This was the city whose gates he uprooted and carried off (Judg. 16.1-3); this was the city, too, where he was subsequently put to hard labour, after he was captured by the Philistines, 'eyeless in Gaza, at the mill with slaves'. It was in Gaza that he wreaked his final vengeance on the Philistines when he pulled down the temple of Dagon on them and on himself.

Canaanite Gaza had been the base for Egyptian operations in that part of the world; when the Philistines settled there it was the most southerly of their five cities. The site of Old Testament Gaza lies about three miles inland, in the north-eastern section of modern Gaza. Gaza was certainly known to David, although it is not named in the history of his reign.

Ashdod is also unnamed in the history of David's reign. It too was an ancient Canaanite city; its site is marked by Tell Ashdod, three and a half miles south-east of modern Ashdod.

Ekron receives a single mention in the story of David: after the downfall of Goliath, the exultant Israelites put the Philistines to rout and pursued them from the Valley of Elah, south-west of Jerusalem, 'as far as Gath and the gates of Ekron' (1 Sam. 17.52). It is provisionally identified with the ruined site called Khirbet el-Muqanna, north-east of Ashdod, where remains of a city wall and some Philistine and Israelite pottery have been found.

The ruins of the Philistine city of Ashdod are covered by coastal sand hills.

Biblical references 1 Samuel 17.4; 2 Samuel 21.15-22 – Gath: the home of Goliath and other giants.
2 Samuel 15.19-22 – Gath: the home of Ittai, David's loyal follower.
1 Samuel 21.10-15 – David loses his nerve as he approaches Gath and gets away by pretending to be mad.
1 Samuel 27.2,3 – David approaches Gath with greater confidence and receives a warm welcome from the king.
2 Samuel 5.17-25 – David conquers the Philistines and makes them subject to his authority.

A twisted tree amid the ruins of Old Testament Bet Shean (Bethshan). The red sky reflects the tragedy of the defeat of King Saul on nearby Mount Gilboa, and the display of his armour on the walls of Bethshan.

The Mediterranean.

Hebron

Haram el-Halil, 'The Enclosure of the Friend' – the great shrine erected over the Cave of Machpelah, reputed burial place of the patriarchs.

Hebron (earlier called Kiriath-arba) was David's residence for the first seven years of his reign (2 Sam. 2.11). After Saul's death in the battle of Mount Gilboa, David consulted the oracle (which was in the custody of the priest Abiathar) to find out where he should make his headquarters, and was directed to go to Hebron. To Hebron accordingly he went, with his family and his seasoned guerrilla band, and there he was visited by the leaders of the tribe of Judah, who anointed him as their king (*c.* 1010 B.C.). Hebron was a suitable site for the capital of the kingdom of Judah: it lay in the heart of the tribal territory, some twenty miles south-south-west of Jerusalem. Then, as now, it was well supplied with springs of water. There David's first six sons were born.

For the first two years David was king of Judah only. Saul's surviving son Eshbaal (whose proper name, usually changed by

scribes to Ish-bosheth, is preserved in 1 Chron. 8.33) took over his father's title as king of Israel, but because the Philistines controlled the territory on the west bank he had to set up his capital at Mahanaim, east of the Jordan. But Eshbaal's power rapidly dwindled. First he foolishly quarrelled with his uncle Abner, his commander-in-chief. Abner in rage came to Hebron to make his peace with David. He was treacherously murdered by Joab and received a state funeral at Hebron, with David as chief mourner. Then Eshbaal himself was assassinated. The assassins, naively imagining that David would reward them for getting his rival out of the way, brought the dead man's head to Hebron and were put to an ignominious death for their pains. Eshbaal's head received burial in Abner's tomb (2 Sam. 4.12).

There was no one fit to take Eshbaal's place, so, two years after Saul's death, the elders of Israel, remembering how at one time David had been a popular and successful military commander under Saul, came to him at Hebron and anointed him king over all Israel (2 Sam. 5.1-3). Hebron was too far south to be a suitable capital for the kingdom of all Israel, but David stayed there until he captured Jerusalem in the seventh year of his reign and established his capital there.

David's position as king of Judah had been tolerated by the Philistines, who thought his power-base too weak to be a threat to them; besides, there was constant war between David's followers and the followers of Eshbaal, and they hoped that both sides would be worn down by the fighting. But when David became king of all Israel, they recognized an impending challenge to their control of the country. War broke out between them and David, in which David ultimately gained the upper hand, compelling the Philistines to acknowledge him as their master.

Hebron viewed from the upper room of one of the houses.

Modern Hebron is a bustling Arab city, a centre of Arab national consciousness.

After David established his capital in Jerusalem, Hebron plays little part in the story of his reign until Absalom's rebellion, when David had been king for about thirty years. It was the men of Judah in particular that Absalom patiently and subtly seduced from their allegiance to his father, and it was by design that Absalom chose Hebron, the chief city of Judah and his own birthplace, for the raising of the standard of revolt: 'Absalom is king in Hebron!' (2 Sam. 15.10).

After the disruption of the monarchy which followed Solomon's death, Hebron was one of the cities of Judah which his son Rehoboam fortified for the defence of his reduced kingdom (2 Chron. 11.8). It then disappears from Old Testament history. The name of the city appears on jar-handles of the 8th century B.C., in the inscription 'Belonging to the king: Hebron'. From this it has been inferred that there was a royal pottery there. Presumably it was one of the cities of Judah taken by Sennacherib in 701 B.C. (Isa. 36.1). After the fall of the kingdom of Judah in 587 B.C. it was taken over by the Edomites (Idumaeans), with most of the Negev, although in Nehemiah's day (445 B.C.) some of the people of Judah are said to have lived 'in Kiriath-arba and its villages' (Neh. 11.25). It was captured from the Idumaeans by Judas Maccabaeus in 164 B.C. (1 Macc. 5.65). Under Herod the Great, himself of Idumaean origin, it was embellished with fine buildings, especially on the sites of Mamre and Machpelah. It was destroyed by the Romans in A.D. 68 while they were reducing the Judaean rebellion.

Hebron figures in the story of the patriarchs. Abraham lived for long periods at Mamre, one and two-third miles north of Hebron, and he bought the cave of Machpelah, with the field in which it was situated, to be a burying-place for his wife Sarah (Gen. 23). There he himself and the patriarchs of the next two generations were buried in turn (Gen. 49.31). The modern city of Hebron, indeed, is built around the site of the patriarchs' tombs (contained within the sacred enclosure Haram el-Halil, the 'Enclosure of the Friend'). The biblical Hebron was situated on the hill er-Rumeideh, just west of modern Hebron; that, in fact, remained the site of Hebron until Crusader times.

The name Hebron means 'federation'; it probably goes back to the time, rather later than Abraham's day, when several settlements in the neighbourhood joined forces to become one city. There appear to have been four of these settlements, if one may judge by the alternative name of Hebron – Kiriath-arba (Gen. 23.2), 'city of four' or, as we might say, tetrapolis.

The narrative of the spies in Numbers 13.22 tells how, moving in from the southern wilderness, 'they went up into the Negev, and came to Hebron; and Ahiman, Sheshai, and Talmai, the descendants of Anak, were there'. Then a note is added informing the reader that 'Hebron was built seven years before Zoan in Egypt'. This chronological note may have been crystal-

The Arab market-place in modern Hebron, a hive of activity on market days.

clear to its first readers, but it is not so clear to us. Which building of Zoan is meant? Several successive cities, with different names, were founded on the site ultimately occupied by Zoan (Tanis), the modern San el-Hagar. Since the name Zoan (Tanis) is not attested before the 11th century B.C., one of the earlier foundations on the site is probably intended – perhaps Avaris, set up by the Hyksos invaders in the eastern Delta when they entered Egypt about 1720 B.C. If so, then the federated city of Hebron was established shortly before that, probably as a Hyksos fortification.

The Anakim, or 'descendants of Anak', who controlled Hebron during the Israelites' wilderness wanderings, are reputed to have been exceptionally tall: their name may mean 'the long-necked people'. They were dispossessed by Caleb, who claimed the region for himself and made good his claim by conquering it (Josh. 14.6-15). Caleb was a Kenizzite, member of a clan which perhaps belonged originally to that locality and was in due course adopted into the tribe of Judah. The neighbouring citadel of Debir or Kiriath-sepher ('city of books') was also taken by Caleb's men; his nephew Othniel, who led the successful assault on it, was rewarded by receiving Caleb's daughter Achsah as his wife (Josh. 15.16,17; Judg. 1.12,13).

At a later date in the period of the judges, it was to the hill east of Hebron (thirty-eight miles away) that Samson carried the gates of Gaza (Judg. 16.3). Presumably they were pointed out on the summit of the hill in the narrator's day. Nothing is recorded of the fortunes of Hebron from its capture by Caleb until the reign of David, except that (together with Kedesh-naphtali and Shechem) it was one of the three 'cities of refuge' established west of the Jordan (Josh. 20.7).

Biblical references Genesis 13.18 – Abraham settles near Hebron.
Numbers 13.22 – The twelve Hebrew spies come to Hebron and find the sons of Anak there.
Joshua 14.6-15; Judges 1.20 – Caleb captures Hebron and acquires it as his family possession.
2 Samuel 2.4,11 – David anointed king of Judah at Hebron; he reigns there for seven and a half years.
2 Samuel 15.7-10 – Absalom proclaims his revolt at Hebron.

Parts of the masonry of the *Haram el-Halil* date back to Herodian times.

Gibeon

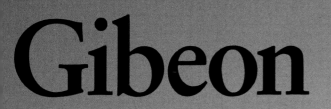

The hill of el-Jib, modern site of the ancient city of Gibeon. The site, about six miles north of Jerusalem, has been excavated in recent years.

The name of Gibeon is preserved in the modern el-Jib, a village seven or eight miles north-west of Jerusalem. Any doubt that might once have existed about the identity of the two places was removed during excavations on the site in 1956 and 1957, when many jar-handles were found inscribed with the name Gibeon.

Gibeon in Canaanite days was 'a great city, like one of the royal cities . . . and all its men were mighty' (Josh. 10.2). It was the leader in a federation of four cities (the other three being Chephirah, Beeroth and Kiriath-jearim) inhabited by an ethnic group called the Hivites (Josh. 9.7,17). When they heard of the victorious approach of Joshua and his army, the Gibeonites hastily sent ambassadors to enter into treaty relationship with them, pretending to live a long way off from those Canaanite cities against which the Israelites had launched a holy war. When their subterfuge was discovered, the treaty had already been sworn and could not be revoked, but the people of Gibeon were reduced to the status of serfs – 'hewers of wood and drawers of water for the house of my God', said Joshua (Josh. 9.23). The implications of their becoming temple-servants for the Israelites were more far-reaching than could have been foreseen at the time.

The news of the Gibeonites' defection prompted four Canaanite kings in the neighbourhood, headed by the king of Jerusalem, to attack them and, if possible, wipe them out. The Gibeonites sought the protection of their new allies, the Israelites, who inflicted a crushing defeat on the united Canaanite army in the pass of Beth-horon, a few miles north-west of Gibeon. It was on this occasion that the sun 'stood still' over Gibeon, so that daylight was prolonged to enable the Israelites to complete their victory (Josh. 10.12-14). This 'strange deed' accomplished in 'the valley of

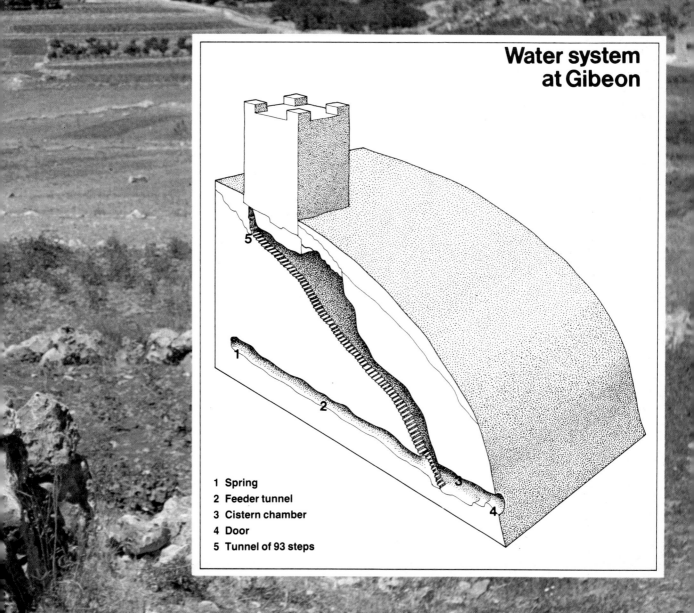

There was an elaborate water system at Gibeon. A rock-cut water chamber could be reached by means of a spiral staircase. An Iron Age tunnel, with ninety-three steps, led to a spring outside the city wall.

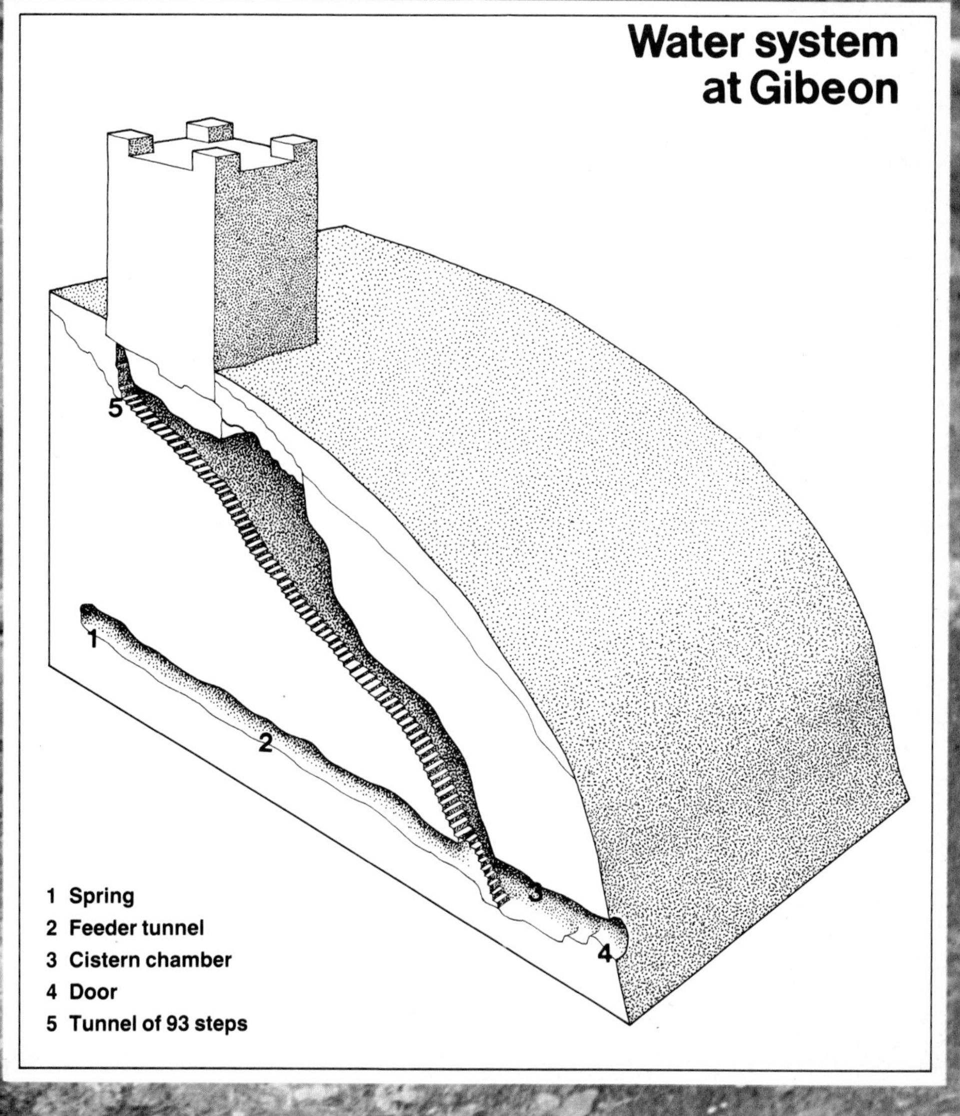

Part of the spiral staircase around the shaft cut in solid rock leading to the underground pool at Gibeon.

Gibeon' was remembered centuries later (Isa. 28.21).

In the allocation of the land among the tribes of Israel, Gibeon fell to Benjamin's lot (Josh. 18.25), but its revenue, together with that of the surrounding pastures, was reserved for the priests.

After the settlement no more is heard of Gibeon until the reign of David. It was the scene of a sanguinary encounter in the fighting that went on for some time between David's followers and the followers of Saul's son Eshbaal, who had been proclaimed king of Israel in Transjordan. Eshbaal's followers, led by his uncle Abner, met David's followers, led by his nephew Joab, at the pool of Gibeon (2 Sam. 2.14). This great rock-cut pool, on the north side of Gibeon, was discovered and cleared out in 1957. It is a cylindrical cutting, 37 feet in diameter and 35 feet deep, with a spiral staircase of 79 steps on the north and east sides leading down to the bottom of the pool and into a tunnel which gives access to a water-chamber lying at a depth of a further 44 feet. The original excavation of this pool must have involved the removal of some 3,000 tons of limestone.

It was agreed between the two commanders that the issue should be settled that day between twelve young men from either side. Each killed his opposite number, so that all twenty-four fell dead. For that reason, we are told, the place was known as Helkath-hazzurim, 'the field of sword-edges' (2 Sam. 2.16). Since the issue remained undecided, the two main bodies of soldiers joined battle and David's men routed their opponents. Joab's young brother Asahel, 'as swift of foot as a young gazelle', tried to win renown for himself by chasing Abner with the hope of killing him; Abner advised him to turn back but, when he refused to listen, it was Asahel who was killed by Abner. Joab did not forget this, and when Abner, some time later, came to make peace with David at Hebron, he in turn was killed by Joab (2 Sam. 3.27).

A similar incident took place nearby some thirty years later, 'at the great stone which is in Gibeon' when Joab killed Amasa, whom David had appointed commander-in-chief in Joab's place after the crushing of Absalom's rebellion (2 Sam. 19.14; 20.8-10).

But most macabre of all the events associated with Gibeon was the exposure of the bodies of seven sons or grandsons of Saul 'before the Lord at Gibeon on the mountain of the Lord' (2 Sam. 21.6). This was a means of expiating the blood-guilt incurred by Saul (and, through him, by his family) because he had put Gibeonites to death in breach of the covenant made in Joshua's day. The Israelite law, that such bodies should be buried before sunset, was evidently not observed by the Gibeonites, and the bodies of the seven men remained exposed for weeks, if not for months. There is a desperately moving picture of Rizpah, Saul's concubine and mother of two of the dead men, guarding their bodies from beasts and birds of prey until David, hearing of her devotion, decided that honour had been served and gave the bodies decent burial, together with the bodies of Saul and his three sons who died with him on Mount Gilboa, which he fetched from Jabesh-gilead, in their ancestral tomb.

This story shows, more clearly than any previous reference to Gibeon in the Old Testament, that Gibeon, with its 'mountain of the Lord', was a sacred site. This was probably the hill on which stood 'the great high place' or sanctuary where Solomon offered sacrifice in the earlier part of his reign and where God appeared to him in a dream and invited him to ask whichever gift he chose (1 Kings 3.4-14). In 1 Chronicles 21.29 the pre-eminence of the high place at Gibeon is explained by the preservation there of the wilderness tabernacle with its altar of burnt-offering (*cf.* 1 Chron. 16.39; 2 Chron. 1.3-6).

The excavations at el-Jib in 1956 and following years have brought much more to light than the great pool. Another, and later, means of access to water in time of siege was a tunnel with ninety-three steps leading through the mountain from inside the city wall to the spring outside which serves the village to this day.

The inscribed handles of wine-jars which confirmed the identity of el-Jib with Gibeon were but part of a variety of evidence that under the Judaean monarchy the place was a centre for the production, storage and export of wine. The winery contained wine-presses hollowed out of the rock. When the wine was bottled, it was stored in sixty-three rock-cut cellars which preserved it at a constant temperature of 18 degrees centigrade. There was storage space for 25,000 gallons of wine.

Mention is made in another Old Testament story of the 'great pool' (literally 'great waters') at Gibeon. When Ishmael son of Nethaniah murdered Gedaliah, the governor whom Nebuchadrezzar placed over Judah after the fall of the monarchy (587 B.C.), he rounded up the surviving members of the royal family and others who had been left in Gedaliah's custody at Mizpah, a mile or two north of Gibeon, and compelled them to follow him and his men to the king of Ammon, in Transjordan. But at the pool of Gibeon they were met by a patriotic leader, Johanan son of Kareah, who liberated Ishmael's captives and eventually took them to safety in Egypt (Jer. 41.10-18).

The last reference to Gibeon in the Old Testament strikes a more cheerful note: men of Gibeon receive honourable mention for their co-operation in building the wall of Jerusalem under Nehemiah (Neh. 3.7; *cf.* 7.25).

Biblical references Joshua 9 – The people of Gibeon make a covenant with the Israelites.

Joshua 10.12-14 – The sun 'stands still' at Gibeon.

2 Samuel 2.12-32 – The battle at the pool of Gibeon.

2 Samuel 21.8-14 – Expiation of covenant-breaking at Gibeon.

Jeremiah 41.11-16 – Rescue at the pool of Gibeon.

Jerusalem

The Jerusalem that David knew was the city which he and his followers captured from its Canaanite inhabitants in the seventh year of his reign (*c*. 1003 B.C.) and in which he thenceforth resided as his royal capital.

Jerusalem has a history going back many centuries before David's time. Part of it, indeed – the upper part of the valley of Rephaim (where the south-western suburbs of the city now lie) – was settled in prehistoric times.

David's Jerusalem lay south of what became the temple area: it was the well-fortified settlement on the south-eastern hill called Zion or Ophel (2 Chron. 27.3; 33.14; Neh. 3.26,27; 11.21). Ophel is a ridge about 1,300 feet long from north to south and 500 feet broad from west to east, with an area of about twelve acres. It was protected on the west by the Tyropoeon valley (the valley of the 'cheesemakers'), on

King David conquered the Jebusites, who occupied the site of Jerusalem, and erected his city on Mount Ophel to become the political and religious centre of his kingdom.

the south by the valley of Hinnom and on the east by the Kidron valley. It lies outside the wall of the Old City today. There was continuous settlement here from the Early Bronze Age (*c*. 2800 B.C.).

The population of Jerusalem is said in Ezekiel 16.3 to have been of mixed ancestry – partly Amorite (Semitic) and partly Hittite (non-Semitic). Its name is first recorded in Egyptian inscriptions of the 19th and 18th centuries B.C.; it appears later in the Tell el-Amarna tablets, part of the archives of the Egyptian foreign office between 1387 and 1362 B.C. The form which its name takes in those tablets, Uru-salim, means 'the foundation of Shalem'. Shalem was a Canaanite divinity mentioned in the cuneiform texts from Ugarit (Ras Shamra) in the 14th century B.C. At a later date the second part of the name was equated with the Hebrew word *shalom*, 'peace', and the whole was interpreted as 'city of peace' (compare Heb. 7.2, where 'king of Salem' is

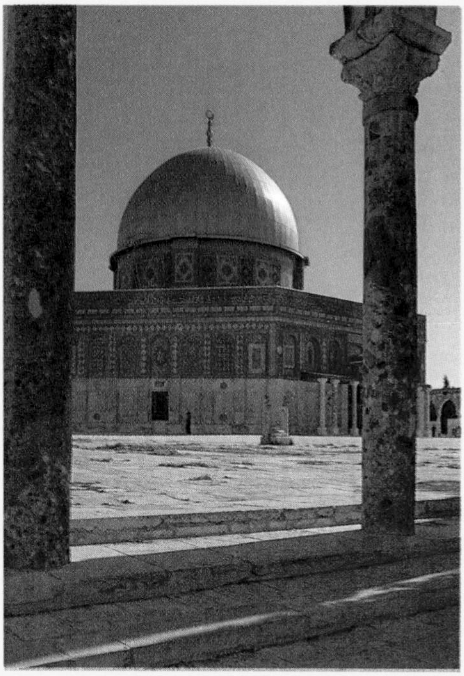

The Dome of the Rock stands over the area where Solomon's Temple was constructed c 950 BC.

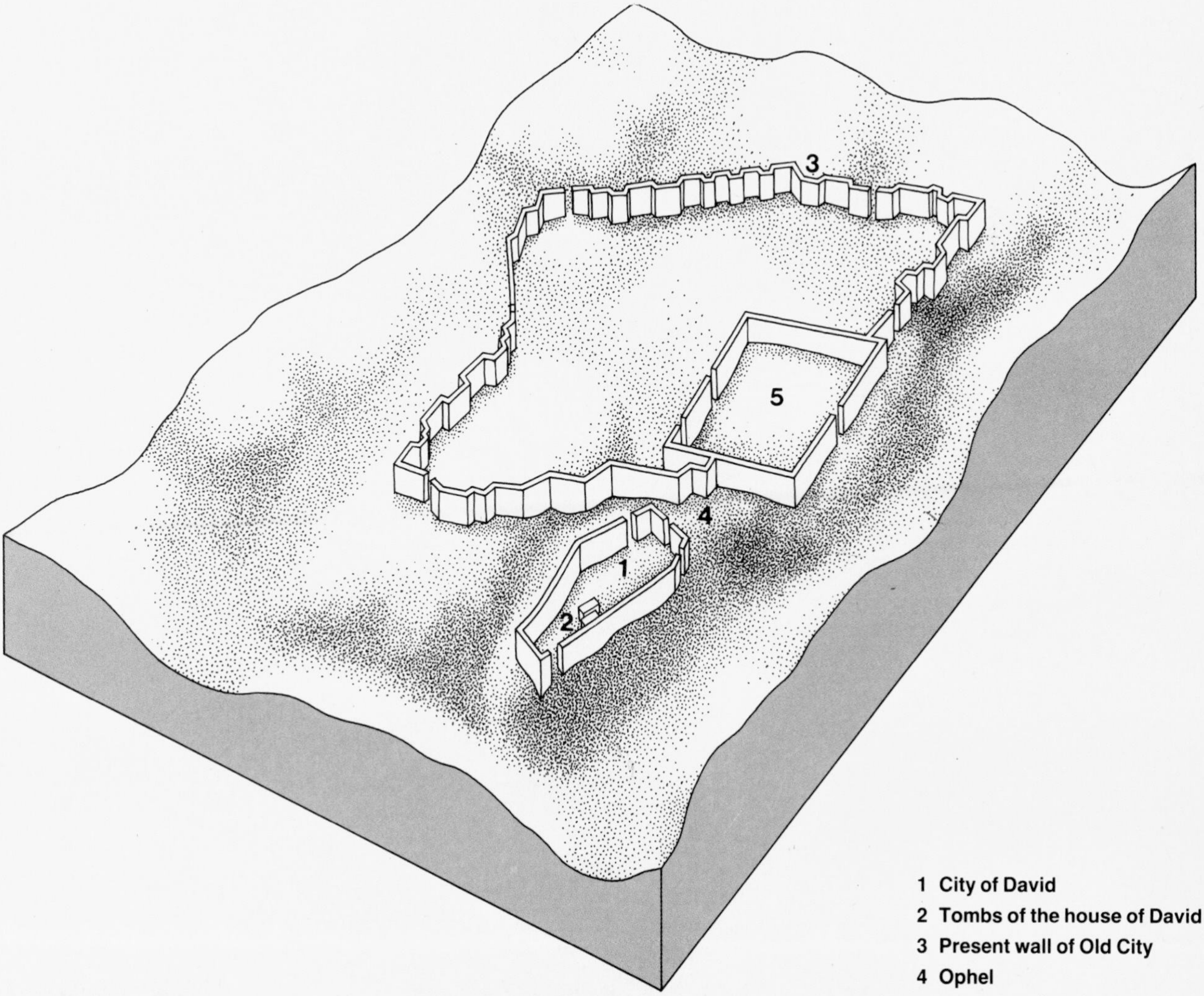

1 City of David
2 Tombs of the house of David
3 Present wall of Old City
4 Ophel
5 Temple area

1 City wall
2 Underground spring
3 Way in to tunnel from city
4 Possible forced entry

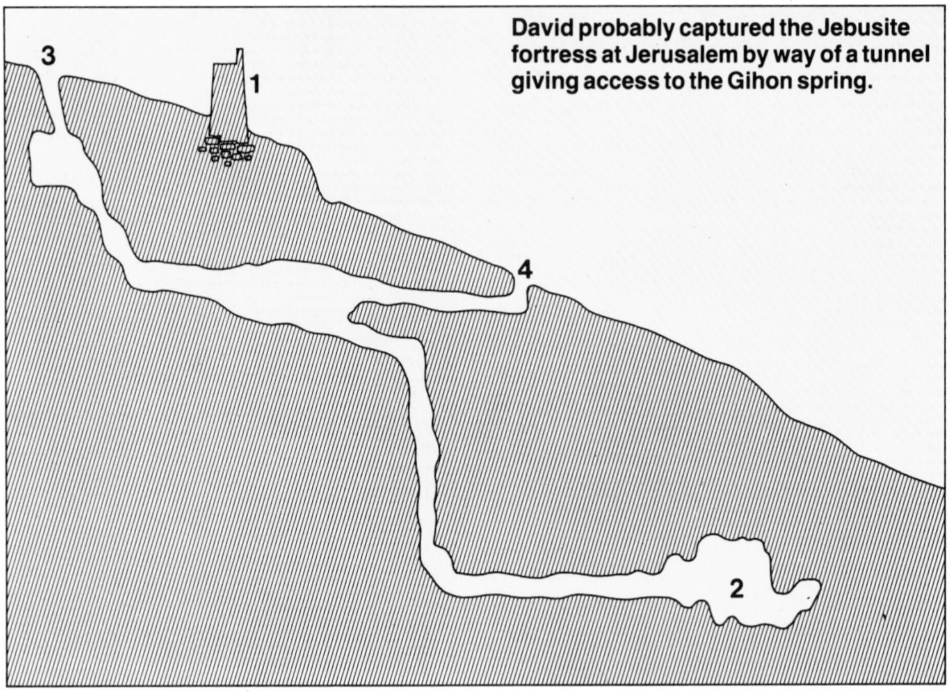

David probably captured the Jebusite fortress at Jerusalem by way of a tunnel giving access to the Gihon spring.

said to mean 'king of peace').

From the Tell el-Amarna tablets it appears that Jerusalem was at that time part of the Egyptian empire in Asia; its ruler, Abdi-hepa, was a vassal of Pharaoh. The tablets include six letters to Pharaoh from Abdi-hepa, who protests his total loyalty. 'Behold, this land of Jerusalem', he says, 'neither my father nor my mother gave it to me; the mighty arm of the king gave it to me.' But he is distressed because some of his opponents are sending the king slanderous reports casting doubt on his loyalty. He is also vexed by the marauding activities of people called the Habiru – quite possibly the same word as 'Hebrews', although we can scarcely identify them with the invading Israelites under Joshua.

Even today orthodox Jews come to the Western Wall or Wailing Wall to remember the desolation of the Temple.

The earliest reference to Jerusalem in the Bible probably mentions it under the shortened name Salem. When Abraham returned south from his defeat of the kings from the east who had invaded the Jordan valley, the king of Salem, Melchizedek, met him with a gift of bread and wine and bestowed a priestly blessing on him; he in turn received from Abraham one tenth of the spoils of war (Gen. 14.18-20). The identity of Salem with Jerusalem has been questioned, but it is taken for granted in later parts of the Old Testament, as in Psalm 76.2, where 'Salem' is used as synonymous with 'Zion'. The supreme God was worshipped in Salem under the designation *El Elyon*, 'God Most High', and after David's capture of Jerusalem *Elyon* is used, especially in the Psalms, as an alternative name of the God of Israel. Thus Psalm 92 begins with the words:

'It is good to give thanks to the Lord *(Yahweh)*,
to sing praises to thy name, O Most High *(Elyon)*'

– where the Israelite name *Yahweh* and the Jerusalemite name *Elyon* stand in what is called 'poetic parallelism' the one to the other.

Jerusalem figures briefly in the accounts of the Israelite settlement of Canaan. Adonizedek, king of Jerusalem (whose name is quite similar to Melchizedek's), organised the league of five kings who tried to destroy the Gibeonites for their defection to Israel: he and his allies were defeated by Joshua in the pass of Beth-horon (Josh. 10.12-14). The king of Jerusalem is listed among the kings overthrown by Joshua in Josh. 11.10, but Joshua is not said to have taken Jerusalem. The Jerusalem which the men of Judah are said to have captured and burned in Judges 1.8 may have been a settlement on one of the other hills later incorporated in the city and not the Jebusite fortress of Ophel: that fortress, we are assured, remained uncaptured throughout the age of the judges (Josh. 15.63; Judg. 1.21).

When the Levite and his concubine undertook their northward journey from Bethlehem, their servant suggested that they should spend the first night in the 'city of the Jebusites', but his master said, 'We will not turn aside into the city of foreigners, who do not belong to the people of Israel; but we will pass on to Gibeah' (Judg. 19.11,12). They would probably have fared better in Jebusite Jerusalem than they did in Israelite Gibeah; they certainly could not have fared worse.

Even when the Philistines established control over much of the territory in the neighbourhood of Jerusalem, Jerusalem seems to have preserved its independence,

Solomon's Temple

an artist's reconstruction

1 **Holy Place**
2 **Holy of Holies**
3 **Ark of the Covenant**
4 **Bronze pillars**

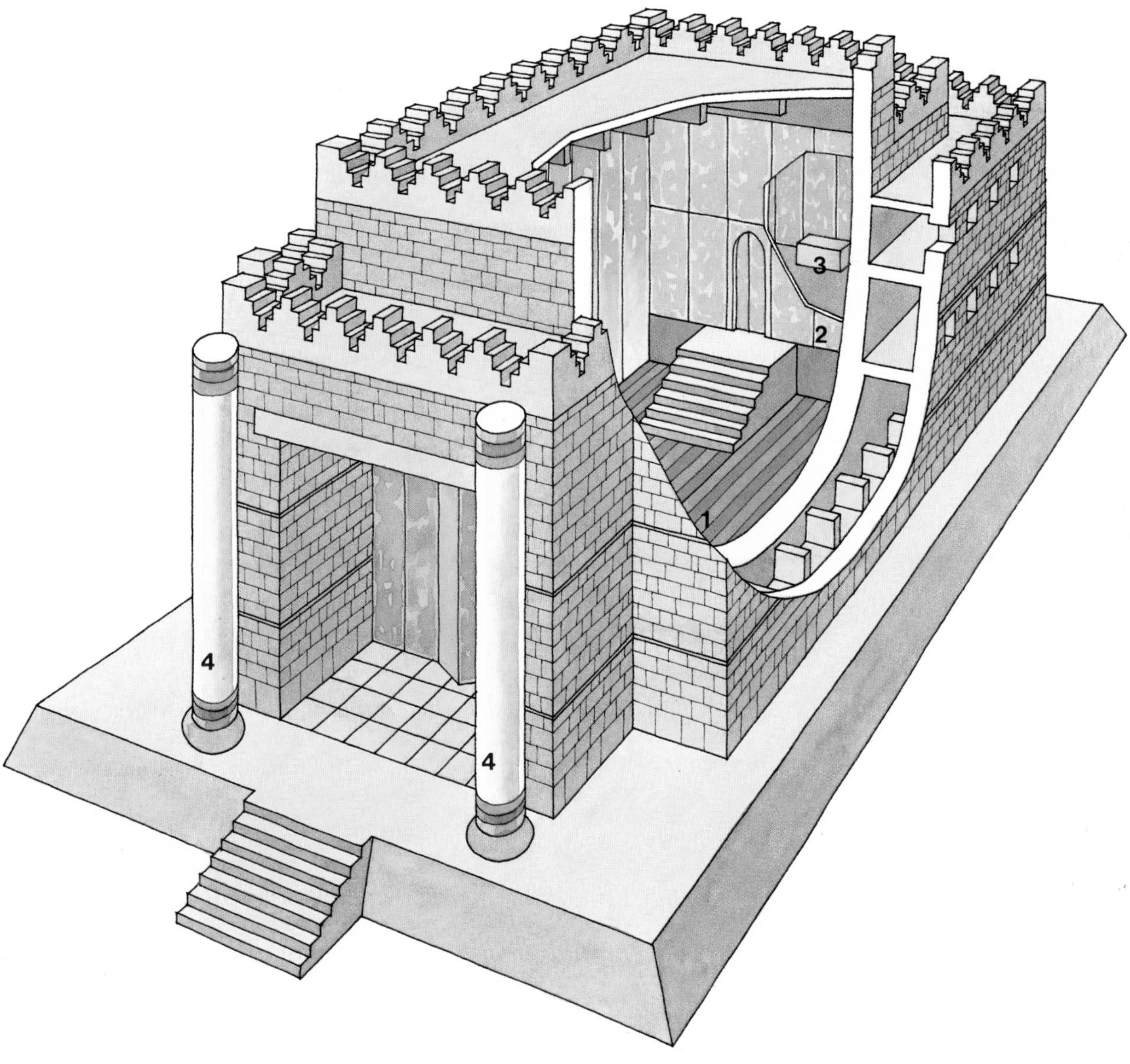

and it continued to do so until the time of David. The credit for capturing the city is given to Joab in 1 Chron. 11.6. The means by which he captured it is disputed: much depends on the meaning of the Hebrew word *sinnor* in 2 Samuel 5.8. If RSV is right in translating it 'water shaft', then Joab seems to have led a party of men up the shaft by which water was brought through the rock from the spring Gihon (today the Virgin's Fountain) in the Kidron valley into the city – a feat which the Jebusites evidently discounted as impossible. They were taken by surprise: before they knew what was happening, David's men held the city.

Houses crowded together in the Kidron Valley, also known in the Bible as the Valley of Jehoshaphat.

There was no wiping out or eviction of the population. David made Jerusalem his capital, and it came to be called 'the city of David', 'David's burg', as James Moffatt translated it (2 Sam. 5.9). He enlarged and further fortified the place: the 'Millo' ('filling') of 2 Sam. 5.9 perhaps denotes the terraces on the east slope of Ophel which formed supporting walls for the royal palace – the 'house of cedar' (i.e. the house panelled with cedar) of 2 Sam. 7.2 – and other new buildings.

In this view of the old city of Jerusalem, the Temple area and the Mount of Olives beyond, can both clearly be seen.

From every point of view David's choice of Jerusalem as his capital was wise. Its strategic strength (which can be gauged from the succession of lengthy sieges which it sustained) was turned to David's advantage. It provided a centre from which he could dominate the land and complete his conquest of the Philistines.

Politically it was helpful to have a capital which belonged to neither part of his united kingdom. David was first elected king of Judah (2 Sam. 2.10,11) and only subsequently king of Israel (2 Sam. 5.1), and there was constant tension between the two, which resulted in their splitting apart after Solomon's death (1 Kings 12.16-20). But neither Israel nor Judah could complain that David favoured the other in his choice of a capital.

Jerusalem remained for some time a separate city-state: David was king of Judah, Israel and Jerusalem. In Jerusalem he may have had himself installed as successor to the ancient dynasty of priest-kings to which Melchizedek had belonged in Abraham's day: the importance of Melchizedek to David's dynasty is reflected in the oracle of Psalm 110.4: 'You are a priest for ever after the order of Melchizedek'. At David's death it was not his oldest surviving son Adonijah (born in Hebron) who succeeded him, but Solomon, a younger son, who had the advantage of being a native of Jerusalem.

Jerusalem became the religious centre of David's realm also when he brought the ark of the covenant out of the obscurity in which it had remained since its capture and restoration by the Philistines a generation or more before (1 Sam. 4.11-6.16). The ark was the palladium of the twelve tribes; it symbolized the presence of the God of Israel in the midst of his people, and the shrine where it was kept was traditionally their central sanctuary. It had moved about from time to time, but from David's time it remained in Jerusalem until the city and temple were destroyed by the Babylonians in 587 B.C.

David housed the ark in Jerusalem in a special tent (2 Sam. 6.17). This was in accordance with tradition: it had been housed in a tent when it was first constructed during the wilderness wanderings. But David felt increasingly that a mere tent provided unfit accommodation for the ark, so he planned to build a temple worthy of the ark and of the God whose presence it symbolised. The word of God through the prophet Nathan, however, forbade him to carry out the plan, while expressing appreciation of the thought that prompted it. The task of building a temple was reserved for his son and successor, Solomon; towards the end of his life David began to make preparations for the temple which Solomon was to build.

To the north of Ophel lay the site which, from Solomon's time onward, became the temple area. It was probably a sacred precinct already. Tradition indeed identifies the rocky outcrop covered today by the Dome of the Rock with the spot where Abraham raised an altar to sacrifice his son Isaac (Gen. 22.9). But it is difficult to pinpoint the particular mountain in 'the land of Moriah' where Abraham was directed to offer up Isaac; it may or may not have been the 'Mount Moriah' on which, according to 2 Chronicles 3.1, the foundations of Solomon's temple were laid. It is said in 1 Chronicles 21.28-22.1 that David decreed

Tombs in the Kidron Valley, which the Jews expect to be the site of the Last Judgment.

that the temple, and more particularly the altar of burnt-offering, should be set up on the threshing-floor of Ornan the Jebusite (called Araunah in 2 Sam. 24.16-25). From this man (perhaps the former Jebusite king) David bought the threshing-floor because the angel of the Lord appeared to him there.

The city on Ophel continued to expand under David and Solomon, especially towards the north, to link up with the temple area. But it was not until the reign of Hezekiah (about 700 B.C.) that part of the territory to the west of the Tyropoeon valley (marked by the street el-Wad, which bisects the Old City as a north-south axis) was settled and surrounded by a wall. This wall, of which remains have come to light in recent years, is possibly referred to as 'another wall' in 2 Chronicles 32.5. The area which it enclosed is probably the district known in Josiah's reign (639-609 B.C.) as the 'Second Quarter' (2 Kings 22.14).

Biblical references Genesis 14.18-20 – The city of Melchizedek (compare Hebrews 7.1-10).
2 Samuel 5.6-10 – The city of David.
Psalm 48.2 – The city of the great King. (The 'great King' is God; compare Matthew 5.35.)
Psalm 87.5,6 – The city of the first-born ones (compare Hebrews 12.22,23).
Psalm 122 – The city of pilgrimage.

Consider the features of Jerusalem which make it a model for the 'Jerusalem above' which 'is free, and she is our mother' (Galatians 4.26), and for 'the holy city, new Jerusalem, coming down out of heaven from God' to be his dwelling-place with men and women (Revelation 21.2,3).

Kiriath-jearim

Kiriath-jearim, 'the city of woods', lying about eight miles west of Jerusalem, is first mentioned in the Bible as one of the four cities of the Gibeonite federation (Josh. 9.17). Later it was included in the tribal territory of Judah. It is mentioned occasionally under the names Baalah (Josh, 15.9-11), Kiriath-baal (Josh. 15.60) and Baale-judah (2 Sam. 6.2), which probably indicate that it was at one time a centre of Baal-worship.

Its importance in the story of David is bound up with the fortunes of the ark of the covenant. The ark was taken from its shrine in Shiloh in the days of Eli (*c.* 1050 B.C.) to go before the Israelite army when it fought with the Philistines at the first battle of Ebenezer (1 Sam. 4.1-11). Far from guaranteeing victory, the ark was captured by the enemy, its two priestly custodians (the sons of Eli) were killed, and the Israelites suffered a crushing disaster. But the ark caused such havoc in the Philistine cities that its captors were forced to return it, and it found a resting-place for many years at Kiriath-jearim, in the house of Abinadab 'on the hill' (1 Sam. 7.1) – probably overlooking the village from the north-west. Eleazar, a son of Abinadab, was consecrated to be its attendant.

Israel might never have recovered from its catastrophic defeat by the Philistines but for the personality of the prophet Samuel, who exercised priestly and judicial functions, and led the people in national repentance. When at last their morale was restored, they defeated the Philistines on the very battle-field of Ebenezer where they had been routed twenty years before (1 Sam. 7.5-14). But Samuel in his wisdom did not restore the ark to its former central place in national life. Instead of putting their trust in the living God, the people had treated the ark as a talisman ensuring their safety, and it had let them down. Under Samuel's guidance they looked directly to

Arab boys.

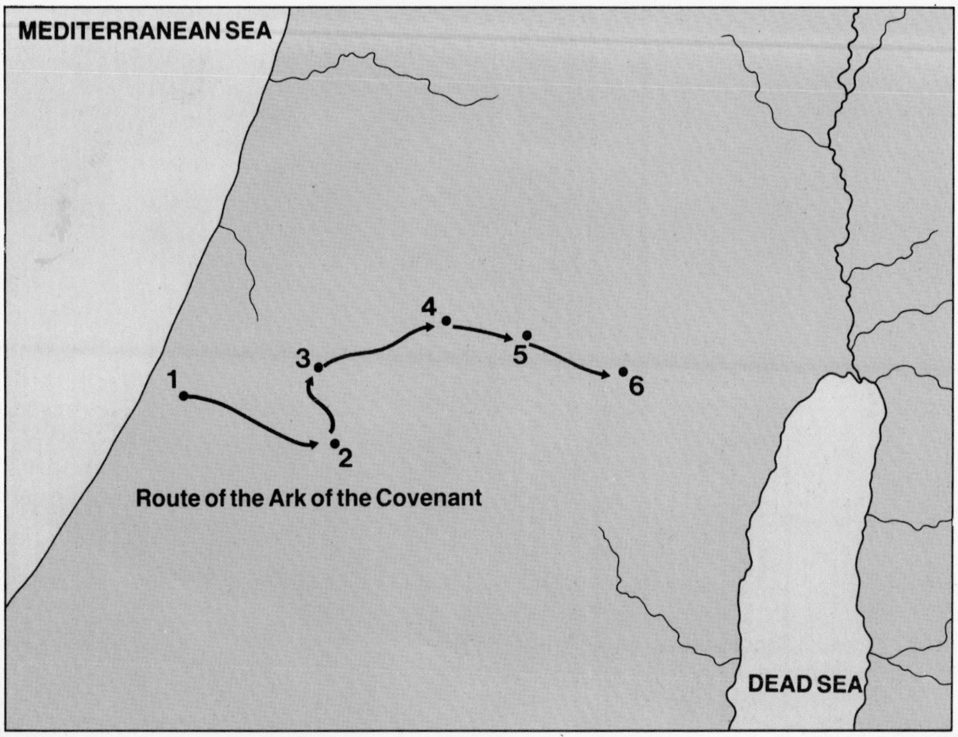

1 Ashdod
2 Gath
3 Ekron
4 Beth-shemesh
5 Kiriath-jearim
6 Jerusalem

God, and forgot about the ark.

When David captured Jerusalem and made it his capital, he did all he could to enhance its prestige, and one thing he did was to construct a tent-shrine for the ark and fetch the ark from Kiriath-jearim to be installed on Mount Zion. The ark had once been the symbol of Yahweh's presence at the centre of the nation's life, and David planned to reinstate it in its former centrality. His first attempt to bring it to Jerusalem was attended by misfortune: Uzzah, one of the sons of Abinadab, fell down dead when he touched the ark to steady it, and the installation was postponed to a more propitious occasion. At the second attempt all went well.

The fetching of the ark from Kiriath-jearim is commemorated in one of the Psalms which celebrates God's choice of David as his anointed and of Mount Zion as his abode – for 'the fields of Jaar' (or 'the fields of the wood') in Psalm 132.6 should probably be understood of the district around Kiriath-jearim. The psalmist recalls how David vowed to give himself no rest until he had established 'a dwelling-place for the Mighty One of Jacob', and goes on (verses 6-8):

Lo, we heard of it in Ephrathah,
we found it in the field of Jaar.
'Let us go to his dwelling-place,
let us worship at his footstool!'
Arise, O Lord, and go to thy resting place,
thou and the ark of thy might.

Kiriath-jearim was rebuilt and resettled after the return from the Babylonian captivity (Neh. 7.29) but plays no further significant part in biblical history – unless the Crusaders were right in identifying the Emmaus of Luke 24.13 with the locality now occupied by the village of Abu Ghosh. Abu Ghosh most probably marks the site of Kiriath-jearim, but the Crusaders' identification of the site with Emmaus rests on no

The Arab village of Abu Ghosh, biblical Kiriath-jearim, where the Ark of the Covenant was lodged for twenty years before King David took it to Jerusalem. In the foreground is the Crusader church built to commemorate the Emmaus story.

The countryside near Kiriath-jearim.

The Arab village of Abu Ghosh, near the site of Old Testament Kiriath-jearim.

There is an impressive church at Kiriath-jearim to mark the site of the biblical events which took place there.

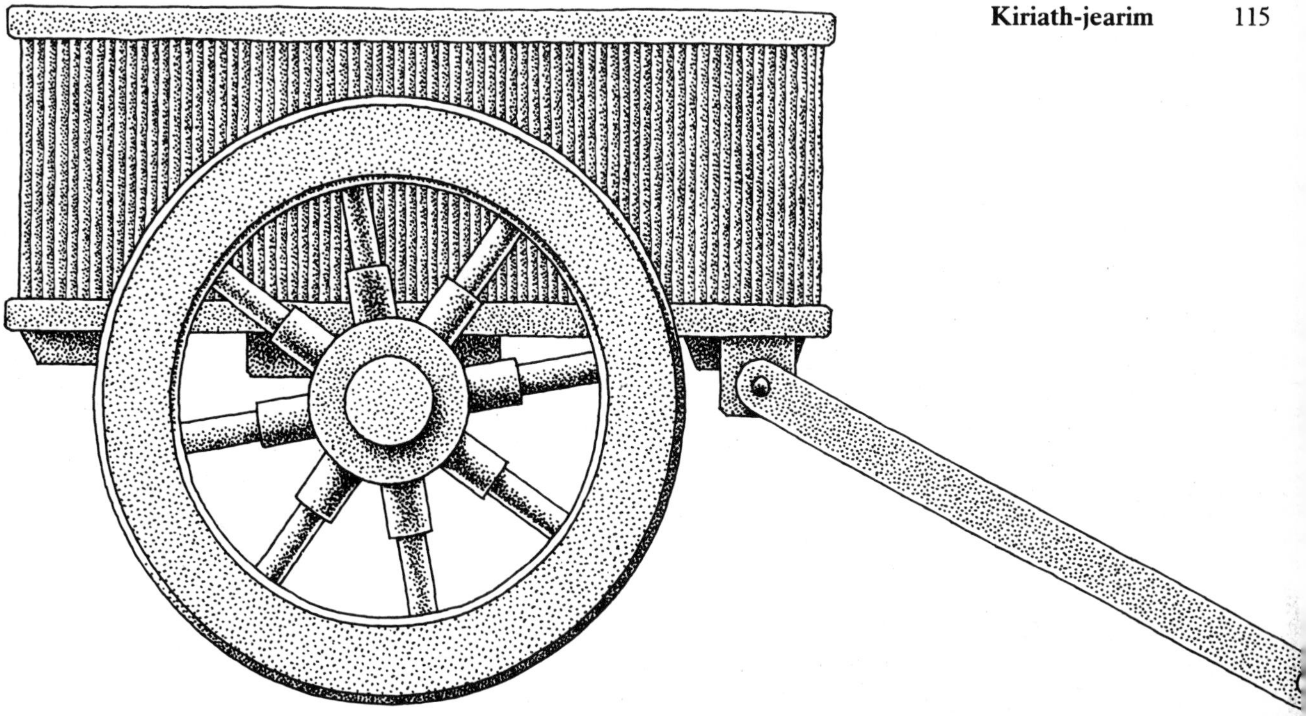

An artist's impression of an Israelite waggon similar to that in which the Ark of the Covenant was conveyed.

more positive foundation than its lying at the appropriate distance from Jerusalem – about sixty furlongs, as Luke says. The Crusaders built a church there in 1142; it was restored by the French in 1899. Into its wall was built a stone which bears the stamp of the Tenth Legion, the Roman force which guarded the derelict site of Jerusalem and its environs after A.D. 70.

What is believed to be the site of Abinadab's house has been covered since 1924 by the Josephine Convent of the Ark. The commemoration of the ark has come to be linked with the veneration of the Virgin Mary. (So far as tradition is concerned, it is Ain Karim or En Kerem, four and a half miles south-west of Jerusalem, held to be the birthplace of John the Baptist, that claims to be the place where Mary visited Elizabeth and sang her hymn of praise – a claim commemorated there by the Church of the Magnificat.) As for Abu Ghosh, it is not unfitting that the place which once accommodated the symbol of God's presence with his people should be associated in religious thought with her in whose womb the Word became flesh in order to dwell among us.

Biblical references 1 Samuel 6.21-7.2 – The ark kept at Kiriath-jearim.
2 Samuel 6.1-5 – The ark fetched from Kiriath-jearim (Baale-judah).
Psalm 132 – The finding and reinstatement of the ark.
Nehemiah 7.29 – Kiriath-jearim repopulated after the exile.

Jericho

Jericho appears to have been at one time a centre of moon-worship; its name is clearly derived from the Canaanite and Hebrew word for 'moon'. It was not a city in David's day, but it was a place he knew – a frontier-post of his kingdom, on the west bank of the Jordan, only a few miles north of the point where the river flows into the Dead Sea.

The Tell of old Jericho, opposite the well of Elijah – or Sultan's Well (Ain es-Sultan). Archaeologists have driven a deep trench across the hill to investigate the successive layers of settlement.

Inset: Excavations of the Canaanite tower at the Tell of old Jericho.

Jericho is mentioned once only in the biblical record of David's reign. David had a long-standing alliance with Nahash, king of Ammon in Transjordan. When Nahash died, David sent ambassadors to express his condolences with his son and successor, Hanun, and to wish him well in the kingship to which he had succeeded. But Hanun, like other inexperienced youths in the Old Testament narrative who found themselves suddenly promoted to high office, listened to the most foolish advisers. They told him that David's ambassadors had ulterior motives in coming to his court, that they were really spies who would report back to David such weaknesses as they saw in his capital city Rabbath-Ammon (modern Amman). Hanun seems to have had no clue about the kind of man David was: he went beyond the limit of insanity in treating his ambassadors with contempt, cutting their garments short and shaving off half their beards, leaving one side of the face smooth and the other fully

This view gives a clear indication of the size of the Tell and the extent of excavations.

bearded. In another culture David, on learning his ambassadors' plight, might have told them to shave off the rest of their beards, but that was not acceptable in the culture to which he and his men belonged. What he said was, 'Remain at Jericho until your beards have grown, and then return' (2 Sam. 10.5; 1 Chron. 19.5).

Jericho was near the fords of the Jordan and was thus a convenient place for the men to stay until they were fit to make a public appearance. It may have been by one of these fords that David, a few years later, crossed the Jordan when he fled from Absalom's rebellion (2 Sam. 17.22) – the place of his crossing is not named, but as he left Jerusalem by way of the summit of the Mount of Olives (2 Sam. 15.30), the most natural direction for him to take was the Jericho road.

No doubt there was some kind of human settlement at Jericho in David's day. It could hardly be otherwise, for Elisha's Fountain (Ain es-Sultan) pours forth fresh water at a thousand gallons a minute, and has been doing so for thousands of years. Such a water supply was not to be neglected. But there had been no walled city of Jericho since the destruction wrought by Joshua and his army at the end of the Late Bronze Age, at least two centuries before David, nor did a walled city rise there again until 'Hiel the Bethelite built Jericho' anew in the days of King Ahab (873-852 B.C.). Archaeological examination of the site suggests that this new Iron Age city must have been a small-scale affair, and indeed the biblical narrator indicates that Hiel's building operations were dogged by disaster. In the later part of the Judaean monarchy, however, the site – Tell es-Sultan, as it is called by Arabs today – was effectively occupied. But this latest Iron Age Jericho was destroyed on the eve of the Babylonian captivity. When the wall of Jerusalem was broken through by the

The Mount of Olives can be seen in the distance from the slopes of the sheep fields outside Bethlehem.

The view across the Jordan valley from the site of ancient Jericho.

Babylonian siege-engines, King Zedekiah escaped from the city and fled towards Jericho, but he was overtaken and captured 'in the plains of Jericho' (2 Kings 25.5). There was no further occupation of the site. A new Jericho arose in the Persian period two miles south of the ancient city. Tell es-Sultan was left for modern archaeologists to explore.

The barren hills traversed on the lonely road from Jerusalem down to Jericho.

When modern archaeologists did begin to explore the site, they found ample evidence of an earlier and greater Jericho than written records gave any idea of. The two best-known phases of excavation on Tell es-Sultan were those directed by John Garstang between 1930 and 1936 and by Dame Kathleen Kenyon from 1952 to 1958.

Tell es-Sultan is of elongated oval shape: it rises to a height of 70 feet above the surrounding plain and covers an area of over ten acres. The plain of Jericho is about 800 feet below Mediterranean sea level.

Human occupation on the site goes back to Mesolithic times (*c.* 8000 B.C.); this was followed by a Proto-Neolithic stage and that in turn by a Neolithic stage. Neolithic ('New Stone') is the name given to that phase of culture when implements and utensils were still being made of stone but a farming economy had begun to be developed: men were not content to be food-gatherers, as they had been in the Palaeolithic ('Old Stone') Age but began to be food-producers. The Mesolithic Age was a transitional phase between the two. In the earliest Neolithic settlement (*c.* 7000 B.C.) the people of Jericho lived in solid houses of

Sheep and goats take advantage of the shade of a solitary tree in the midday sun at Jericho, said to be the most ancient city in the world.

The Tell of old Jericho, sometimes known as the Tell es-Sultan, site of Old Testament Jericho.

mud brick, in which evidence was preserved of the manufacture of flint and bone tools and of limestone utensils. A regular town wall followed, with a great stone tower built against its inner side on the west.

A second Neolithic phase was marked by houses more elaborate and sophisticated in style. Their walls were made of elongated mud bricks with a herring-bone pattern of thumb-impressions. They were covered, as were the floors, with a coat of burnished lime-mortar. The rooms were rectangular, and grouped around an inner court in which was a fireplace. The people who lived in these houses, like their predecessors of the earlier Neolithic phase, buried their dead beneath the floors of their houses.

But the most striking discovery of this phase of settlement was that of ten human skulls with their features restored in flesh-tinted plaster, the eyes inlaid with shells. This presumably has some bearing on the beliefs of the community, but what that bearing might be it is difficult to say.

Both these Neolithic phases antedated the introduction of pottery. The first pottery found at Jericho belongs to a later phase of the Neolithic Age. The people who first used pottery on the site lived in other respects at a lower cultural level than their predecessors; their dwellings were huts, in contrast to the mud-brick houses of the pre-pottery Neolithic phases.

The Bronze Age saw the rise and fall of several successive cities, starting about 3000 B.C. Before archaeologists had perfected their dating techniques, it was possible to ascribe Early Bronze fortifications to the Late Bronze period. When it was claimed in the 1930's that the fallen walls of Joshua's Jericho (the Late Bronze city) had been discovered, the walls in question (as was established later) actually belonged to the Early Bronze Age. Throughout the Bronze Age, Jericho was the point of entry into Canaan for nomadic tribes from the eastern desert. Joshua's directions to his spies, 'Go, view the land, especially Jericho' (Josh. 2.1), must have been anticipated by many leaders in the preceding

centuries.

Early Bronze Age Jericho seems to have been destroyed shortly before 2000 B.C. by a body of invaders from the desert – probably those who settled in Canaan and came to be known as the Amorites. The Early Bronze town wall was destroyed by fire, and a nomadic population pitched its tents on the site for some generations.

Another wave of newcomers arrived about 1900 B.C. and introduced a culture,

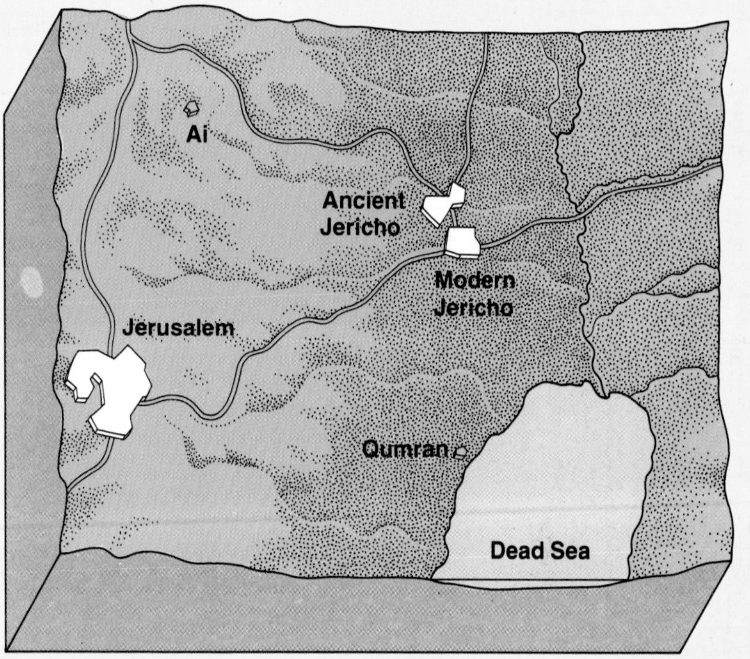

Bedouin traders and farmers bargain over animal prices.

Jericho and the Jordan valley as seen from the Judean Hills to the west.

conveniently called Canaanite, which endured through the Middle and Late Bronze Ages until the disappearance of Jericho about 1200 B.C. There were successive foundations on the site during this period, one at least of which, at the end of the Middle Bronze period (*c.* 1600 B.C.), was destroyed by fire. It is reasonable to associate this destruction with the expulsion of the Hyksos from Egypt: the Egyptians pursued the retreating Hyksos into Asia. It is in the debris of this destruction that we find the clearest evidence of the way of life in Bronze Age Jericho.

Although, as a rule, violent destruction leaves more evidence for the archaeologist than gradual decline, Joshua's destruction of Late Bronze Jericho is an exception. Because of erosion through a period of three and a half centuries before the city was rebuilt, practically nothing remains of Late Bronze Jericho. By David's time the name simply indicated a place where his humiliated amabssadors could wait for nature's restoring process before going up to Jerusalem and showing their faces in public.

Biblical references Joshua 6.26 – Joshua's curse on the rebuilding of Jericho.
1 Kings 16.34 – Hiel the Bethelite incurs Joshua's curse.
Joshua 6.25 – Rahab rescued from Jericho. According to Hebrews 11.31 it was by her faith that she was rescued; according to James 2.25, that faith was shown by her 'works' – 'when she received the messengers and sent them out another way'. According to Matthew 1.5, by subsequently marrying a prince of the tribe of Judah she became an ancestress of Jesus.
2 Samuel 10.5 – Jericho a frontier-post of the kingdom of Judah.
2 Kings 25.5 – Zedekiah, Judah's last king, captured in 'the plains of Jericho'.

Rabbath-Ammon

One of the most important of the military exploits of David's reign in non-Israelite territory was the siege and capture of Rabbah, the capital city of the kingdom of Ammon (2 Sam. 11.1; 12.26-31).

Rabbah of the Ammonites (Deut. 3.11 etc.) or Rabbath-Ammon remains a capital city to this day: it is modern Amman, capital of the Hashemite kingdom of Jordan. Rabbah means 'great', so 'Rabbah of the Ammonites' is 'the great (city) of the Ammonites'.

The Ammonites, like their kinsfolk the Moabites, were established as a settled community in Transjordan shortly before the Israelites arrived in that area towards the end of their wilderness wanderings. The Israelites did not clash with the Ammonites at that time; they were in fact divinely forbidden to harass them (Deut. 2.19). They did, however, invade and occupy the territory of the Ammonites' neighbour, Sihon king of the Amorites, whose residence at Heshbon was about fourteen miles south-west of Rabbath-Ammon. Another Transjordan ruler whom the Israelites defeated and dispossessed at that time was Og, king of Bashan, the only survivor of the 'Rephaim', whose gigantic 'bedstead of iron', nearly 14 feet long by 6 feet wide, was preserved in later days as a museum piece in Rabbath-Ammon (Deut. 3.11). (The NEB makes the object a 'sarcophagus of basalt' instead of an iron bedstead.) How it found a resting-place in Rabbath-Ammon, many miles south of Og's homeland, we are not told.

The Rephaim were a people that in early days occupied that part of Transjordan where the Ammonites and Moabites later settled. The Moabites called them Emim and the Ammonites called them Zamzummim (Deut. 2.10,20,21). Middle Bronze Age objects found by Italian archaeologists between 1927 and 1933 near the top of the acropolis of Rabbath-Ammon and in

The chief town of the Ammonites was Rabbath-Ammon, modern Amman.

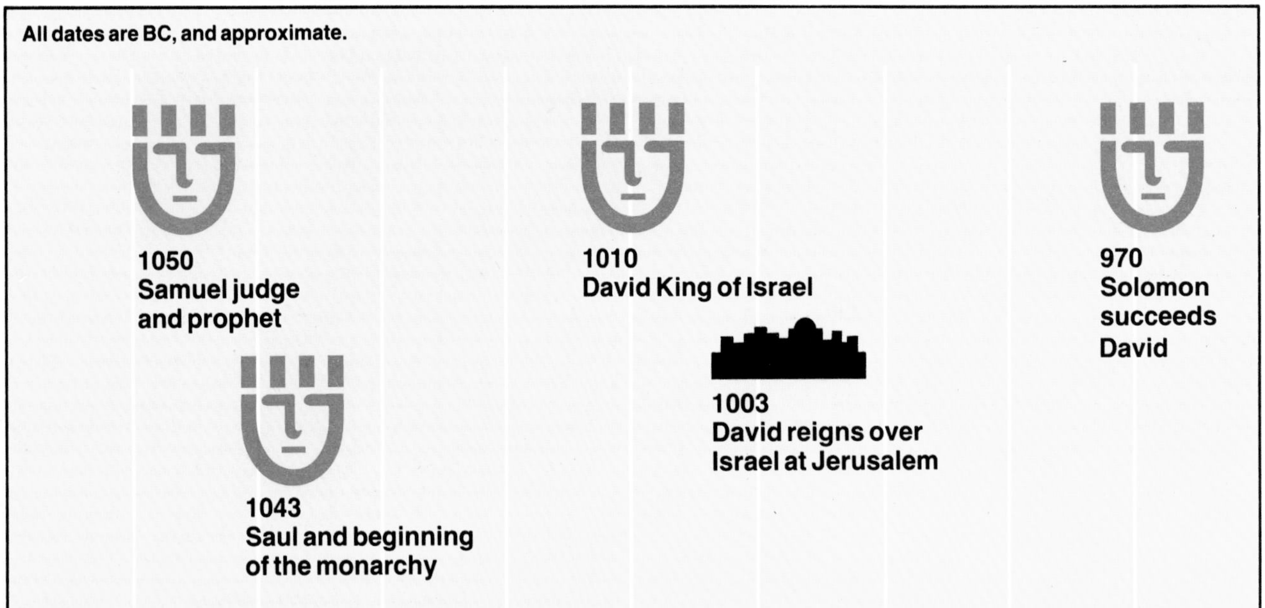

The first Kings of Israel

tombs in the neighbouring Jebel Qal'ah may be relics of this earlier occupation, as may also walls of the upper terrace of the acropolis.

In 1955, during extensions to Amman airport, a small Late Bronze Age temple, 46 feet square, was discovered. It was examined at that time by G. Lankester Harding and excavated in 1966 under the direction of J. B. Hennessy. Hennessy thought that the temple was founded at the end of the 14th century B.C. and abandoned in the 13th century, which may suggest that it belonged to the latest phase of the pre-Ammonite period. On the middle terrace of the upper city Italian archaeologists discovered what may have been a rock-altar of Milcom, the principal god of the Ammonites. A few inscriptions from the 9th and 7th centuries B.C. present the only known remains of the Ammonite language, which (like the Moabite language, known from King Mesha's 'Moabite Stone', found at Dibon in 1868) was closely akin to Hebrew.

Rabbath-Ammon was built in a well-watered region, at some of the headwaters of the River Jabbok, which flows into the Jordan from the east.

If the Israelites did not clash with the Ammonites at the end of their wilderness wanderings, they did clash with them several times in the next two or three centuries. The rise of Jephthah, who 'judged' the Transjordanian Israelites for six years, was due to Ammonite encroachment, which did not stop at the Jordan, but pressed into central and southern Canaan, 'so that Israel was sorely distressed' (Judg. 10.9). In their extremity the people turned to Jephthah, a half-Israelite leader of outlaws, and begged him to take command: he did so, and defeated the Ammonites.

At the beginning of Saul's reign Nahash, king of the Ammonites, threatened to enslave the Israelites of Jabesh-gilead. They sent an urgent message to Saul, asking for help. He mustered the military strength of Israel and by forced marches reached Jabesh-gilead in time to deliver its people, and routed the Ammonite army (1 Sam. 11.1-11). This military exploit did much to secure Saul's acceptance as king. At a later date Nahash entered into a treaty-relationship with David; but when David took steps to renew the treaty with Hanun, son and successor to Nahash, his ambassadors were insulted – a clear indication on Hanun's part that the treaty had lapsed. Such an insult was not to be tolerated: David declared war on the king of Ammon and his army besieged Rabbah. The siege was directed by Joab, David's commander-in-chief. It was during this siege that Uriah the Hittite was killed, having been posted by David's orders 'in the forefront of the hottest fighting' (2 Sam. 11.18).

The siege was long, but the city fell at last. The lower city, 'the city of waters' (so called presumably because it guarded the water supply) was taken under Joab's command, and he sent a curt message to David bidding him take charge of the reduction of the upper city (the acropolis) –'lest I take the city', said Joab drily, 'and it be called by my name' (2 Sam. 12.28). What Joab thought of David's staying behind in Jerusalem with Bathsheba may be readily guessed. So David took command of the final stage of the siege, and the upper city fell. The citizens were put to forced labour, and the crown of Ammon was placed on David's head.

The Ammonite royal house was not exterminated. Shobi, a brother of Hanun, showed his loyalty to David at the time of Absalom's rebellion (2 Sam. 17.27). Among Solomon's wives was Naamah, an Ammonite princess, for whom he built a shrine in honour of the god Milcom (1 Kings 11.1,5,7) and whose son Rehoboam succeeded Solomon on the throne (1 Kings 14.21). After the disruption of the Hebrew monarchy the Ammonites regained their independence.

The Ammonites, like the other small nationalities in that part of Western Asia, were harassed by the Assyrians and Babylonians. They are mentioned as paying tribute to Sennacherib, Esarhaddon and Ashurbanipal. The Ammonite king Baalis (*cf.* Jer. 40.14) rebelled against Nebuchadnezzar at the same time as Zedekiah, king of Judah; Ezekiel depicts Nebuchadnezzar, at the parting of the ways, casting lots to decide whether he should move first against Jerusalem or against 'Rabbah of the Ammonites', and drawing the lot for Jerusalem (Ezek. 21.18-23).

In the 3rd century B.C. Rabbath-Ammon was refounded as a Greek city by Ptolemy Philadelphus of Egypt (285-246 B.C.) and renamed Philadelphia, after him. Under this name it was included in Graeco-Roman times among the cities of the Decapolis. But its earlier designation was not forgotten, and modern Amman preserves the name of the ancient people of Ammon, whose history was interwoven with that of the Israelites, not least in the reign of David.

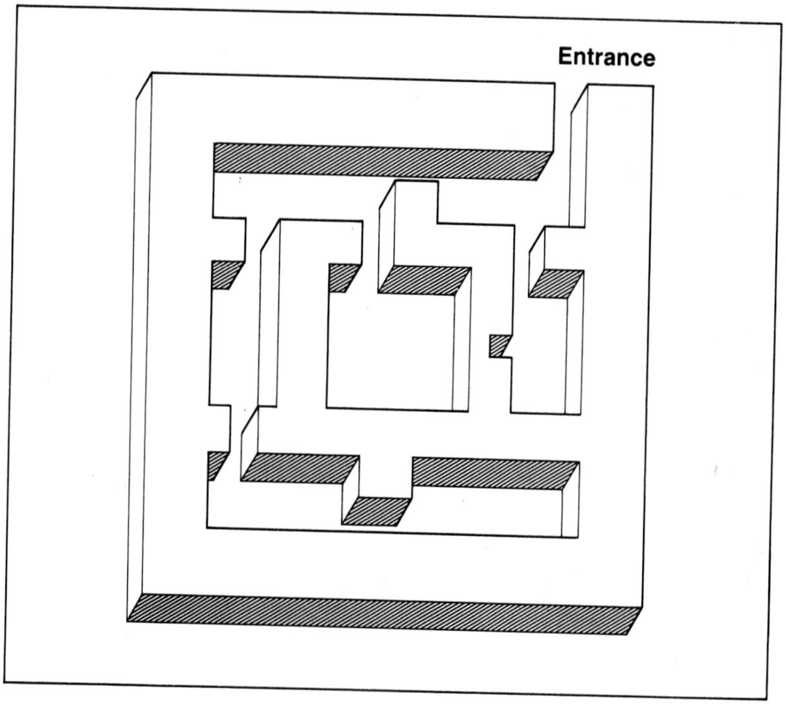

Plan of the Bronze Age temple discovered at Amman.

Biblical references Deuteronomy 3.11 – Og's bedstead (or sarcophagus) preserved at Rabbath-Ammon.
2 Samuel 10.1-5 – David's ambassadors to Rabbath-Ammon insulted.
2 Samuel 12.29 – Rabbath-Ammon captured by David.
Ezekiel 21.20 – Rabbath-Ammon marked for destruction by Nebuchadnezzar.

Index of illustrations: David

Index of illustrations: Abraham

Acknowledgments

Designer: Peter Wyart, Three's Company

Picture Editor: Tim Dowley

Illustrations: James Macdonald

Photographs:

Alia 13, 60 inset, 69

J C Allen 34–35, 77, 100, 102, 104, 125

CMS 63

Tim Dowley 46, 58–59, 60, 88, 90 top, 94, 110, 114

Israel Government Tourist Agency 53

A Neilson 1, 21, 22, 24, 25, 26, 27, 30, 31, 32, 41, 42, 43, 44, 45, 49, 54 top, 55, 56, 61, 74 right, 79, 82–83, 83 bottom, 122

Scripture Union 7, 9, 10, 15 bottom, 20, 28, 33, 34, 37, 38, 39, 40, 47, 48, 49, 50, 51, 52, 54 bottom, 62, 65, 70, 71, 72, 73, 75, 81, 82, 83 top, 86, 87, 89, 92–93, 99, 106, 108, 109, 113, 116, 117, 118, 119, 120, 123 top, 124

Jamie Simson 5, 6, 8, 11, 12, 15 top, 16–17, 18, 57, 76, 84, 90 bottom, 92, 93, 112, 114 inset, 123 bottom

Syrian Embassy 16, 17

Peter Wyart 74 left, 78–79, 91, 96, 97, 98, 111